COME EMPTY

Pour Out Life's Hurts and Receive God's Healing Love

By
Saundra Dalton-Smith M.D.

SonRise Devotionals
Lighthouse Publishing of the Carolinas

PRAISE FOR *COME EMPTY*

Come Empty is full of raw, real, and relevant spiritual insights. It is a rare devotional that challenges you to look deep within your soul while simultaneously lifting your eyes to Jesus. Saundra Dalton-Smith writes in a way that encourages those who are hungry and thirsty for hope to draw near to the Father. This marvelous book has my highest recommendation.

~ **Kurt W. Bubna**
Pastor and author, *Epic Grace: Chronicles of a Recovering Idiot* and *Mr. & Mrs.: How to Thrive in a Perfectly Imperfect Marriage*

Are you hurting? Are you hopeless? Are you empty? Or willing to be? Walk with this servant doctor as she leads hurting hearts on a 50-day journey to let God heal what we're willing to lay at His feet. A loving, daily guide for those needing encouragement to surrender all to Jesus. Inspiring, empowering, and encouraging.

~**Patricia Raybon**
Award-winning author of *I Told the Mountain to Move* and *Undivided: A Muslim Daughter, Her Christian Mother, Their Path to Peace*

Dr. Saundra Dalton-Smith had me crying at page one as compassion pours out through her words. I couldn't put the book down and wanted to dig deeper into the daily devotions. Resisting the temptation, I slowed down and worked through one day at a time for a heart-makeover rooted in Christ. I didn't just read through this book. I prayed through it and journaled my heart. Written in conversational format, the essence is pouring out your heart's cry and listening within your heart for His reply.

~ **Christine Abraham**
Founder and ministry director at WomensBibleCafe.com

We've all had those days when things don't go as planned, when life doesn't make sense. But sometimes we allow the hurt and doubt from those unmet expectations to cloud our hope and joy. In *Come Empty*, Saundra Dalton-Smith encourages us with a fresh, soul-penetrating hope that invites us into a genuine healing experience with God.

~ **Jo Ann Fore**
Author of *When A Woman Finds Her Voice: Overcoming Life's Hurts* and *Using Your Story to Make a Difference*

It's so important to be honest with God and tell Him where it hurts — to pour out your pain to Him, and not keep it bottled up inside, so that you can receive His healing. Dr. Saundra Dalton-Smith's 50 Day Challenge is a wonderful way to focus on reclaiming your emotional and spiritual health.

~ **Christin Ditchfield**
Author of *What Women Should Know About Letting It Go: Breaking Free from the Power of Guilt, Discouragement, and Defeat*

I stand in awe of Saundra's honesty, determination, courage, and relevant spiritual insights. *Come Empty* offers a vision of guidance – where you are invited to share and witness fifty days of inspiring and captivating devotionals, leading you to experience all of the joys and blessings that God has intended for you. Your cup will definitely "run over" after these purposeful devotionals allow you to recognize the love and anointing that God has over your life.

~ **Angelia L. White**
CEO and publisher *Hope for Women Magazine*

Are you drained? Worn out? *"Come Empty"* is an invitation for you to join Saundra Dalton-Smith as she offers you a new outpouring of God's spirit. As a physician, Dalton-Smith is used to asking her patients: "Show me where it hurts." Using this same format, she openly and candidly discusses how spiritual conflicts affect physical health. Bluntly sharing personal prayers from her own painful journey in the "Your heart's cry" sections for each devotional, readers are summoned to face their aches and losses. As hurt and pain are spilled out, spiritual refilling begins with a gentle response from Jesus in the "His reply" sections. If the reader wants to go even deeper, there are more opportunities to do so. The book's practical accessibility through the 50 daily devotions makes it a handy tool for women on the go. Tough, tender, revealing, and healing, you will want to buy an extra copy of *"Come Empty"* to give to someone you love who needs to be refilled.

~ **Sheryl Giesbrecht**
Syndicated radio host, global influencer,
International speaker and author of
Get Back Up: Trusting God When Life Knocks You Down

Dr. Dalton-Smith skillfully conveys God's message of healing and restoration in her newest release *Come Empty: Pour Out Life's Hurts and Receive God's Healing Love*. She masterfully weaves together a collection of devotionals that show us Jesus Christ is acquainted with our struggles and in Him we can remain undefiled before the world. Let this physician, led by the wisdom of the "Great Physician," help you experience God's restorative power in your situation. I highly recommend this book!

~ **Dianna Hobbs**
Award-winning publisher of *EEW Magazine*

Saundra's candid words ring authentic and true because she has lived out every chapter in this masterpiece creation called *Come Empty*. There is one problem with this book: you will have a hard time sticking to the daily reading plan. You will want to devour the book from cover to cover because you know that Saundra's insights hit the deepest longings and aches in your heart. But, she doesn't leave us in our broken places; she helps us to turn to Jesus, the only One who can satisfy our cravings and fill our empty soul. This book is a gift for all of us and I highly endorse it.

~ **Heidi McLaughlin**
International speaker and author of *Sand to Pearls, Making Bold Choices to Enrich your Life* and *Beauty Unleashed: Transforming a Woman's Soul.*

COME EMPTY – POUR OUT LIFE'S HURTS AND RECEIVE GOD'S HEALING LOVE
Published by SonRise Devotionals
An imprint of Lighthouse Publishing of the Carolinas
2333 Barton Oaks Dr., Raleigh, NC, 27614

ISBN 978-1-941103-80-7
Copyright © 2015 by Saundra Dalton-Smith, MD
Cover design: Goran Tomic
Interior design: Karthick Srinivasan

Available in print from your local bookstore, online, or from the publisher at:
www.lighthousepublishingofthecarolinas.com

For more information on this book and the author visit: http://www.drdaltonsmith.com/

Scripture quotations are taken from the HOLY BIBLE NEW INTERNATIONAL VERSION®. NIV® Copyright c 1973, 1978, 1984 by International Bible Society. Used by permission of Zondervan Publishing House. All rights reserved.

Scripture taken from the New King James Version®. Copyright© 1982 by Thomas Nelson, Inc. Used by permission. All rights reserved.

Scripture quotations are from the ESV® Bible (The Holy Bible, English Standard Version®). Copyright© 2001 by Crossway, a publishing ministry of Good News Publishers Used by permission. All rights reserved.

Scripture quotations are from the ESV© Bible (The Holy Bible, English Standard Version©), copyright© 2001 by Crossway, a publishing ministry of Good News Publishers. Used by permission. All rights reserved.

Brought to you by the creative team at LighthousePublishingoftheCarolinas.com: Amberlyn Dwinnell, Cindy Sproles, Eddie Jones, and Shonda Savage.

Library of Congress Cataloging-in-Publication Data
Dalton-Smith, Saundra.
Come Empty – Pour Out Life's Hurts and Receive God's Healing/ Saundra Dalton-Smith, MD
1st ed.

Table of Contents

Identity

Change

Illness

Positive Emotions

Gratitude

Dedication

This book is dedicated to everyone who has ever suffered silently. Know that when you don't have the words to articulate the deep pain inside, God understands every tear and extends an invitation for you to . . . Come Empty.

Chapter 1
The Problem with Pain

"*S*how me where it hurts."

For many years I've made this request of my patients, waiting for them to point to the offending body part causing them physical discomfort. But, sometimes the place where it hurts isn't physical. Sometimes the deepest ache lies in the places no one can see, the places you don't dare to acknowledge for fear of arousing what's already scarred and numb. Yet, healing is only possible when you accept the challenge to break down the scar tissue and exchange its limitations for the flexibility of freedom, resulting in freedom from the pain and its power to control your emotions and thoughts.

So today, I ask you, "Show me where it hurts." Is it the pain of losing a child? Is it the frustration of unanswered prayers? It may be the betrayal of an unfaithful spouse or the shame of being the unfaithful one. Could it be the regret of missed opportunities or overwhelming fear and anxiety about your life and your current situation? Where is the place of your most pressing pain? What life events have left you with an emotional limp? Which loss has taken the most out of you? Show me where it hurts, so together we can move forward into a time of healing and restoration.

An Invitation

Pain is universal. It crosses gender, race, socio-economic status, and education. Pain does not discriminate. Pain is real and it can be debilitating. In my years of practicing medicine, I've yet to encounter someone who enjoys being in pain. As an Internal Medicine physician, I spend most of my time helping hurting people. However, much of the pain entering my medical practice is not the physical type. But rather, it is the emotional and spiritual kind. It is the type of pain that drains the life out of life and leaves you wondering if it is even worth the effort.

Those who come to me with these feelings are not suicidal or bad people. They do not want to feel this way, but life sometimes throws blows at you that seem to take the air out of your lungs. This can leave you feeling like you are drowning without a life-preserver, or any way to stay afloat on the sea of uncertain times. So, the pain becomes the focus, and alleviating the pain becomes the goal. Food, sex, entertainment, drugs, tobacco, and shopping are just a few of the painkillers you may down, trying to soothe the ache and revive your failing heart. And when these vices fail to succeed, life seems even more futile and empty.

It is here in this place of emptiness that you are given an amazing invitation, an invitation to simply come. Not an invitation to become, nor to seek, but rather to bring your stressed-out, worn-out, tired self to the well, brimming with Living Water. It is an invitation to be renewed, strengthened, guided, restored, and satisfied. It is an invitation to live fully, to come empty and be filled.

Southern Exposure

A few years ago, there was a TV show called *Northern Exposure*. In the show, a young doctor was sent to a remote location in Alaska to treat patients as part of a medical equality program. I relate to that show since my own involvement with the National Health Service Corp took me to a small town in Alabama where, as they say in the south, "the rubber meets the road." In my case, the rubber of my scientific, medical education met the road of my spirituality and faith.

Faith was the backbone of the community I lived in. Churches decorated every corner of town, and I could see why the South is called the "Bible Belt." Having grown up in church, I was accustomed to the beliefs but had never imagined my faith and my education would confront each other.

I treated patients daily from all levels of the socio-economic ladder. Teachers, factory workers, radio personalities, and lawyers would come divulge their problems. Some would go as far as bringing a detailed written list of symptoms for me to review. Headaches, back pain, sore muscles, fatigue, dizziness, cloudy thinking, listlessness, nervousness, and restlessness were at the top of the lists. Many were desperate for answers and willing to try anything to find relief. Most had already been on anti-depressants and prescription painkillers, yet failed to find any relief. Many had gone to chiropractors, acupuncturists, or physical therapists, only to get limited results. Almost all had undergone numerous expensive diagnostic evaluations in search of a pivotal diagnosis. They hoped for a definitive treatment, only to be left with huge medical bills from a myriad of negative tests.

Are these people just making this up? I wondered. *Are they all just attention-seekers looking for sympathy? Could it just be in their heads? Are they suffering from depression? Is it menopause? Is it some form of dementia, or are they all just crazy?*

Like many doctors, my frustration with treating these disorders soon turned to cynicism. It's easy to judge someone with these symptoms until you begin to develop a list of your own. Time passed and word spread around town about my "compassionate but straightforward approach." I found myself quickly bombarded with a population of predominately unhappy patients, many afflicted with chronic pain, chronic fatigue, insomnia, anxiety, and depression.

Day-in and day-out, I was confronted with hurting and diseased people in need of a smile, a kind word, some attention, and treatment. No matter how much I poured into the life of one person, it did not help the patient in the next room. So, I poured out more smiles and more kind words, trying to create quality doctor-patient bonds. Eventually, I found myself depleted of reserves. "I've poured it all out in the last exam room," I told my husband one day, "I have nothing left to offer you tonight."

The Crisis of Chaos

You may know the feeling. You wake up and dread the thought of getting out of bed. You find no joy in life and see no point to it. Life becomes one meaningless circle of events where you seem to start and finish at the same point. No victory. No contentment. Life becomes a never-ending race around the same obstacle course. What you once thought of as a career is now merely a job. The child who was once a blessed hope is now your daily trial. There is a heavy weight that seems to have attached itself to you like a leech, threatening to drain you of the blood needed to make it through just one more day.

As time goes on, you begin to have feelings of dread. You anxiously lie in bed, tormented by the events of the day. Sleep evades you like a wayward child. As you reach out to obtain it, it withdraws further away. Pride, moral guilt, and self-preservation cause you to attempt to control these emotions, leaving you with more stress. As you put on a façade of happiness for those around you, you feel like the valve of a pressure cooker, ready to erupt at any moment with the slightest change in emotional temperature. Each day, you go home to your family mentally, physically, and emotionally empty and finding nothing left to offer those you love, except the fragments of what was once a better you.

After years of being a support and guide to a neglected portion of the medical population, I found myself lacking. In many ways, I was worse than the ones who I was sent to assist. I no longer felt I had value or worth, and I carried myself in that manner. I took as little time and pride in my appearance as possible. I mean, what's the point in getting all made up just to exist? I ate whatever I wanted, as much as I wanted, as often as I wanted. Eventually, my 5'2" frame carried 209 pounds. I didn't care about anything. A mundane place of emotional, physical, and spiritual dryness took root.

Every Sunday and Wednesday, I attended church and sang in the choir. I attended Sunday school and led a Bible study in my home. All the while, I was dying on the inside and completely devoid of peace and joy. I knew enough about faith to know I was lacking in some areas, but had no idea how to rectify this. I was doing all I knew to do, with no results.

Days turned to months and months to years as I silently suffered from this condition. Some would have called it depression. Some would have called it chronic fatigue. Some would have classified my chronic neck and back pain as fibromyalgia. Because my pride would not let me go to another physician for treatment, I found myself consulting the Great Physician for answers. Like the Pharisees, I consulted God, not as a servant, but as an equal. *Why is this happening to me? I'm a follower of Jesus Christ, so where is the victory I'm promised? I tithe a tenth of my salary, so why am I not reaping the benefits in Your Word? I have cast my cares upon You, so why do I feel so heavy laden? God, are You there? Do You see how I am suffering? Do You even care?*

In a desperate attempt to hear from God, I found myself going to conference after conference, seeking a word, a sign, anything to help me make it through my life. During the intermission at one conference, my husband and I went to a local restaurant for lunch. A table with five women fellowshipping together caught my eye. These women had a look I'd never seen before. Each possessed a tangible glow of vitality that superseded any medical description I could term. I'm not saying they were all beautiful in a conventional way, but they all had a level of beauty that was supernatural—a genuine contentment that was outwardly evident.

I found myself staring at these women. Toward the end of our meal, I noticed one of them looking in my direction. I quickly averted my eyes and thought to myself, "*Oh goodness, she saw me staring and probably thinks I'm crazy.*" To make matters worse, she walked directly to our table. I was quickly trying to think up some way to explain why I was staring at them, but before I could open my mouth, she began to pray over my husband and I.

By some miracle, that woman sensed we would be receptive to her prayer. In prayer, she addressed issues specific to our current situation. You've heard the term, "*she read my mail.*" Before we could comment, she turned to me and said, "God has seen your tears and heard your cries, and He does care." She smiled, shook our hands, and returned to the table with her companions. My husband and I sat in silence as we absorbed her poignant words. Returning to the conference, I sensed a tangible change in my personal spiritual atmosphere. I contemplated her words and the experience, finding myself drawn to the story of another troubled woman meeting a stranger who had been "*reading her mail.*"

The Woman at the Well

A Samaritan woman was drawing water from a well in her hometown when a Jewish man approached. Since Jews usually did not speak to Samaritans, she was surprised when the man asked her to draw water for Him. The man told her that if she knew who He was, she would ask Him for living water. But the woman was confused. The Jewish man didn't have a bucket, so how would He draw water?

She asked the man, "If you are greater than Jacob, who dug the well?"

The man told the woman her well water would quench her thirst for a while, but He had water that would quench her thirst forever! The woman liked that. She wouldn't have to carry water every day. She asked how she could get this water. The man told her to bring her husband to see Him. When she replied, "I have no husband," He said, "That's right. You've been married before, but you are not now."

When the woman realized this man knew all about her life, she thought He was a prophet, and asked a common religious question about where to worship. The man, whose name was Jesus, replied, "We must worship in spirit and in truth; that's more important than the physical place. We must worship in our heart." (Paraphrased from John 4:1-42)

Like the Samaritan woman, I had found myself looking for a God-connection in a physical place, diligently trying to find the conference that would change my life. I found myself searching for somewhere to recharge my drained spiritual battery, a place to replenish my depleted cup. During my meditations on this Bible story, one aspect echoed in my mind: "Living Water." If there was one thing I was, it was thirsty. I was thirsty for peace, thirsty for joy, thirsty for hope, thirsty for relief from chronic pain and the disappointments of life.

Of all the possible diagnoses for my years of listless living, thirst had never come to mind. But, as I paralleled the symptoms of physical thirst with the symptoms I was experiencing within, I noticed numerous similarities. Recognizing you have a problem is only half the battle; actually owning your problem and making the necessary adjustments are where victories lie.

Divine Dehydration

After years of wrong self-diagnosis, I ultimately succumbed to the reality that I was thirsty for more of God in my life. I had actually gone far beyond thirst and had reached a level of dangerous dehydration. A divine dehydration, a dryness of soul and spirit that left me without the energy to be a blessing to anyone, least of all to myself or God. I was in desperate need of intervention.

Medically, when I encounter a patient with dehydration, the course of treatment is easy. I supplement their fluid loss with intravenous (IV) hydration. I place a direct portal into their bloodstream and pour into them the missing elements and water they are lacking.

I needed the Living Water that only Jesus could provide and a direct infusion of His presence in my life. I needed a spiritual IV, and I needed it at a rate that would catapult me back to a level of total wellness—physically, emotionally, and spiritually.

Hear Jesus Speak

Jesus told the Samaritan woman that God must be worshipped in spirit and in truth. He concluded we must worship Him in our heart. Although I participated externally in a lot of faith-based activities, I failed to internalize my worship. Outwardly, I knew all the right words, phrases, and praise songs. Inwardly, I had no discipline of my daily personal replenishing visits to the well. I was going to all the right places, but failed to go to the One who actually had what I needed. I had neglected to develop a personal, intimate relationship with the Source of my Living Water: Jesus Himself.

I needed to hear Jesus speak to me just as He spoke to the woman at the well. Amazingly, He always had time for me and welcomed my approach into His presence. His invitation was simply to come empty—empty of pretense, empty of self-sufficiency, empty of strength. So, daily I would return with my empty vessel. At first I felt ashamed. I did not want to be needy, but rather needed. I wanted to be self-sufficient. But, with each trip back to the well of His life-giving Word, I left with the understanding He was more than enough. I found when He pours into emptiness, He gives abundantly. So, I continued returning while journaling the words of hope, peace, and joy He supplied, then taking the overflow back to my thirsty patients to watch them drink deeply.

Within the pages of this book, I share some of the hard emotions I took into His presence. Some of these were my emotions, some were those shared with me by my patients. In each dry place I presented before Him, I could hear Jesus speak. He did not speak audibly, but through the living reality of the Word made flesh. He spoke through the mercy seat of the Old Testament. He spoke through the real life emotions in the Psalms. He spoke through the finished work of the cross. And, He spoke through the visions of Revelations. When Jesus speaks, things happen. Hope is renewed. Purpose is realized. Peace is obtained. Fear is dispelled. Joy is birthed. Healing occurs.

You may be unhappy with your current circumstances: financial burdens, marital strain, family responsibility, and pressures may have left you feeling overwhelmed and in a state of disease. Pain is real, whether it is physical, emotional, or spiritual. The problem with pain is it demands to be relieved. It is here, in this place of seeking relief, that an invitation is presented. It's an invitation to come empty. It is my prayer that you will bring the pain and trials of this life daily into His presence, and let Jesus speak words of healing into every place life has hurt you.

As the deer pants for streams of water, so my soul pants for you, my God. **Psalm 42:1 NIV**

Chapter 2
The 50 Day Jubilee Challenge

What would happen if, for 50 days, you went deep into the places of your greatest pain? What would occur if, instead of coming with an agenda, a list, or a specific request, you came before God's presence, empty in anticipation of being filled? What would happen if you brought your lingering questions and your unanswered prayers to the One you feel is not replying? What benefits would you find in daily communicating with the Prince of Peace, the Healer, the Deliverer, the Lover of your soul? What miracles would be possible if, for 50 days, you made time to spend just five minutes before God, expecting to receive relief, healing, restoration, redemption, comfort, and freedom from past emotional and spiritual wounds?

The only way to find out is to accept this challenge to walk through the wilderness of your past pain on purpose. If you are reading this book, then I think it's fair to say you have some places where the pain remains. You may have buried it alive, but it's still there. Pain demands to be relieved, and how you find relief will determine the ultimate outcome. Scarred or healed. Broken or whole. Empty or filled. Jaded or jubilant.

Why Jubilee?

Jubilee in the Old Testament was a time at the end of a forty-nine year cycle when debts were forgiven, property was restored to rightful owners, and those in bondage were set free. In Isaiah 61, a time of the Lord's favor is foreshadowed, and the coming Messiah's Jubilee is made known.

The Spirit of the Sovereign Lord is on me, because the Lord has anointed me to proclaim good news to the poor. He has sent me to bind up the brokenhearted, to proclaim freedom for the captives and release from darkness for the prisoners, to proclaim the year of the Lord's favor. **Isaiah 61:1-2 NIV**

In Luke 4, Jesus is led into the wilderness to confront the areas He will be tested and tried by the enemy. Weak, tired, hungry, and empty of human strength, He left the wilderness with the divine strength of the Holy Spirit. He accepted the invitation to enter into the wilderness on purpose and walked out overflowing with the spirit of Jubilee. His words in the synagogue echo those of Isaiah and reveal the promises you can expect to receive during the next 50 days.

The Spirit of the Lord is on me, because he has anointed me to proclaim good news to the poor. He has sent me to proclaim freedom for the prisoners and recovery of sight for the blind, to set the oppressed free, to proclaim the year of the Lord's favor. **Luke 4:18-19 NIV**

The Message Bible translations of these passages give

additional insight into the promises of Jubilee. In Luke, the year of the Lord's favor is translated as "the year God will act." The year of the Lord's favor in Isaiah is translated as "the year of His grace." In your pain, know God has a time when He will step in on your behalf to reveal to you His faithfulness. When all your strength seems to be gone, be confident that God's grace is sufficient to sustain you through every obstacle, every disappointment, and every trial. His word is His promise, and it will not return void. Emptiness cannot remain an option in the presence of a loving God, but you alone must make the choice to pursue His presence in the midst of your lingering questions and unanswered prayers. Each promise of Jubilee is worth going through this journey from healing to wholeness.

The Promises of Jubilee

1. Assurance of God's presence in your difficult situations
2. Illuminated vision and perspective on your past emotional blind spots
3. Forgiveness of sins that have held your heart and mind captive
4. Grace to bring your disappointments, fears, and doubts onto holy ground
5. Freedom to fully live in the abundance of God's love

The Challenge

1. For the next 50 days read one devotional each day. They are short and can be completed in five minutes, but I encourage you to set aside extended time in His presence. Your resulting peace and joy are worth the effort.

2. After reading the **Your Heart's Cry** sections of this book, add your own words in a journal, sharing with Jesus what is on your heart.

3. As you meditate on **His Reply,** spend a few moments simply listening for any additional words of healing He has for you personally.

4. Go deeper with the included scripture reading and reflection questions.

5. Conclude your time with a simple prayer.

There are eighty total days of devotions from which you will choose fifty that speak to your personal situation. Sixty of the devotions are based on uncovering your pain. You can start with the first devotion and move forward in sequence, or you can use the topical index to pinpoint the areas of your deepest pain. The last twenty devotions are based on moving from pain to the fulfilling of the promises of Jubilee. Spend 30-40 days working through your pain and the last 10-20 days transitioning into the fullness of all God has for you. Each person is unique and the time needed to heal is an individual process. Allow God's Spirit to guide you as you proceed through the 50 days.

Will You Accept?

Life is full of invitations to come empty. Every time things don't go as planned. Every time death comes unannounced. Every time disappointment rears its head. Every time illness strikes. Every time money is low. Every time your strength is gone. Every time fear tries to dominate. Every time faith is overshadowed by doubt. The invitations are countless. The question is not if you will get an invitation, but whether or not you will come. Will you accept life's invitation to come empty and be filled?

I'm not saying the process will be easy. Some pain in our lives can be so deep it becomes a part of who we are, how we view life, and how we interact with others. These deep hurts can seem like an impossible mountain to move. The good news is you don't need to come filled with faith to experience the promises of Jubilee. You can come empty. God's Word declares that even the tiniest seed of faith is enough. Your part is not to do the mountain moving. Your part is to simply come.

I pray during these 50 days you will sense Jesus walking with you through the wilderness of your past pain. I pray He reveals to you the lashes He received for your healing and the wounds He bears, so you don't have to bear them. I pray He will be your cloud by day and pillar of fire by night as you navigate through the hard places in pursuit of His presence. May you experience the Sabbath rest of dwelling in the arms of The Most High and the freedom of being captivated by His love. It takes time to move from the captivity of pain into a new place of liberty in Christ—time which culminates in a season of Jubilee!

So if the Son sets you free, you will be free indeed. **John 8:36 NIV**

Life's Invitations
Relationship With God

Day 1
An Invitation to Come Empty

*Y*our Heart's Cry

I'm stuck, caught someplace between where I've been and where I desire to be. No direction seems clear, and no path looks right. I don't know how to move forward. Yet, here I am, in need, doubting if this, if You, if anything can help me. What can soothe the longing in my heart? What can ease the fears in my mind? What options are there when my situation seems impossible? What point is there to hope when it appears hopeless? Where should I go for help when I've exhausted all my resources?

It is here, when I'm at the end of my rope, that I can finally see the solitary lifeline of Your presence extended to me. It is here the emptiness, the void, the hollowness becomes most keen. How long has it been since I last turned to You in my time of need? When did my heart grow cold to Your call to draw near? Somewhere between the business of daily life and the desire to find my way, I've taken a wrong turn. Nowhere feels comfortable. No place feels like home. The tension pulling on my heart is my constant reminder that I am no longer enjoying the journey of my life. The sleepless nights remind me of my discontentment. The mounting addictions testify to my need to fill the emptiness inside. I'm tired of trying, and I'm done with denying what is obvious: I need help. I need help to move past this wall of apathy. I need help to go beyond the pain of past disappointments. I need help to get back on track with truly living because currently, everything within me is slowly dying in a state of chronic dis*ease*, fatigue, and regret.

Come, let us return to the Lord. For He has torn us, but He will heal us; He has wounded us, but He will bandage us. **Hosea 6:1 NASB**

His Reply

Sit and allow the breeze of recognition to settle between us. How I long for those days when you would spend time talking to Me about your needs and desires. Not praying for an answer, but rather revealing your vulnerability and child-like trust in My ability to navigate every area of your life. I miss those moments of togetherness, those moments of connection when I would get an opportunity to speak words of love, joy, peace, and happiness into your life. Is it any wonder why life has become so difficult? What good is it for Me to speak when there is no ear listening?

Today, I am extending to you an invitation to return to Me with an ear to hear and a heart to receive. You who are weary and burdened. Come to Me with the wounds, bruises, and cuts life has inflicted. Come to Me with your worries, illnesses, and problems. Come to Me empty of this life, open to be filled with new life.

Come to Me, all who are weary and heavy-laden, and I will give you rest. **Matthew 11:28 NASB**

Scripture Reading: Luke 15

Going Deeper Questions:

1. What did Jesus speak to you through the story of the lost sheep, the lost coin, and the lost son in Luke 15? Which of these parables do you most relate to and why?

2. Do you accept His invitation to come empty daily? How does being invited make you feel? What does it say about His feelings toward you?

Simple Prayer: Here I am God. Meet with me.

Day 2
Barriers to Access

Your Heart's Cry

I feel like my prayers go no further than the thin air escaping from my mouth. Not reaching Heaven, but rather bouncing off an invisible barrier erected to prevent me from experiencing any breakthrough or peace. When did this wall go up, and who commanded its construction? What is the use of trying? Why get my hopes up, only to be let down again? My desire to pray has been lost in the sea of disappointment, deferred hope, and damaged emotions. This wall has not only blocked my prayers, but it has blocked my passion to pursue You. Like water dripping upon a flame, each unanswered prayer kills something inside of me. My heart grows colder with each drop, slowly extinguishing what once was ablaze. I don't know how to pray with faith when my faith appears to only be met with silence.

A bruised reed He will not break and a dimly burning wick He will not extinguish; He will faithfully bring forth justice. **Isaiah 42:3 NASB**

His Reply

Access has never been denied you. Your prayers are forever before Me, but prayers grow best in the fertile ground of a surrendered heart. Surrender your heart. Return to Me those areas of your faith that have been torn down. Return to Me those areas of your heart that have been battered by past hurts.

Return to Me those areas of your hope that have been stricken by unbelief. Return to Me all that separates you from Me. Allow Me to daily remove each bandage as I bring to light the truth of My love. Allow Me to heal each area that needs mending. Allow My presence to come to you like a heavy rain, not to put out a flame, but to clean away all pain. Let it cover and saturate every area of your life. As the rain pours over all in its path, so shall My love pour over you. My rain of love will water the dry areas of your life and revive all that appears to have withered and died. If you will devote this daily time with Me, I will not disappoint you. My love will not fail you.

For the eyes of the Lord are on the righteous and his ears are attentive to their prayer. **1 Peter 3:12 NIV**

Scripture Reading: Hebrews 4:4-11

*G*oing **Deeper Questions:**

1. What unanswered prayers have left the deepest wounds? How have the bandages around these wounds entombed your passionate pursuit of the only One able to truly heal?
2. How did the life of Jesus open the door for you to come boldly before God? What prevents you from daily walking through the open door of access you have available to you?

Simple Prayer: Open my eyes to see the door back to fully loving You, God.

Day 3
Power in Presence

Your Heart's Cry

Standing in the middle of my ordeal, I feel utterly alone. Even when I look for You, I do not see You. I do not feel You. Alienated within the confines of my thoughts and emotions, buried under the debris of my anxiety, lies the part of me that once believed all things work together for my good. Now, I do not have the faith to believe this situation will end in anything other than more pain. Pain is my steady companion. Pain has become the presence walking with me daily, overshadowing all hope and mocking any attempts at joy. My tears have paved a trail in my heart for every time disappointment has visited with me. Where are You God when I need You? My heart aches from the loneliness I feel inside. If You are here, why can't I feel You near?

You will show me the path of life; In Your presence is fullness of joy; At Your right hand are pleasures forevermore. **Psalm 16: 11 NASB**

His Reply

Just because you cannot feel Me does not mean I am not there. Where can you go from My Spirit? Or, where can you flee from My presence? Presence is the state of being within your immediate vicinity. I am wherever you are. I am always available to you, but you are not always conscious of Me. With open arms, I welcome you to experience My presence. Listen for the sound of Me walking through the garden of your day. Do not be afraid, and do not hide yourself from Me. I am near to all those who call upon Me. When you cannot feel Me, call to Me. I have not turned a deaf ear to you. I am a present help in your times of need. Do not wait until you feel Me to ask for My assistance. I am always ready to come to your aid. My presence may not change your situation, but it will always change you. If you want to experience more of My presence, enter in with praise. Not praise for the situation you are in, but praising the outcome you anticipate I am able to bring. Praise is the gateway to My presence that nothing and no one can close. Enter in as often as you desire. May My presence become as real to you today as the air you need to survive.

The Lord is near to all who call upon Him, To all who call upon Him in truth. **Psalm 145:18 NKJV**

Scripture Reading: Psalm 139: 1-17

*G*oing **Deeper Questions:**
1. In what life situations have you felt alone? What painful emotional scars has that sense of abandonment left? Has the situation and your perceived abandonment affected your ability to trust God? Why or why not?
2. What does Psalm 139 reveal about God's feelings towards you as an individual? Since God is always accessible, what do you feel has blunted your awareness of Him? What blankets of comfort have you been cocooned inside of?

Simple Prayer: Surround me with Your presence. Let me feel You drawing near to me, God.

Day 4
Purpose of the Void

*Y*our Heart's Cry

I feel empty on the inside. It's an emptiness that goes deeper than hunger and is more consuming than thirst, leaving widespread desolation in its wake. Famine of spirit, darkness of soul, cloudiness of vision, and nonexistent peace remind me of the void inside. The more I try to fill this void, the deeper the hole and the wider the gap between my current state and my desired contentment. What will fill the space? Comfort foods have provided an external cushion to the pain, but ultimately they fail to comfort. The passionate embrace of another has provided momentary satisfaction, but cannot restore my value or self-worth. Many substances help dull my awareness of the empty space inside, but none have poured in anything of substance. Each has only served to take more out of me. When all my vices have been spent and all my tokens have been played, will there be anything left of me to give, or will the shell that is left only be a hollow reminder of the person I could have been?

You, God, are my God, earnestly I seek you; I thirst for you, my whole being longs for you, in a dry and parched land where there is no water. **Psalm 63:1 NIV**

*H*is Reply

Emptiness is not a hindrance to Me, but an opportunity. In the middle of the void lies capacity. The purpose of the void is to remind you of the untapped capacity within you. I am the Master Potter, and I alone know your full capacity. You were made to be filled to overflowing. Allow Me to reveal to you your capacity to retain all I desire to share with you. Do not withdraw from the emptiness; it is only an invitation to come away with Me and learn what is available to you.

You can try to fill the void with all this life has to offer, but it will only leave you still wanting. I am the only One who can pour into this place of need. In Me is the fullness of all that is good and right, and I extend my portion to you. I allowed Myself to be poured out as a sacrificial offering so you never have to feel empty. Make room in your day for Me. Draw near to Me, and I will draw near to you. Identify the cause of your emptiness, and then open yourself to be filled by Me. It is My desire to not only dwell among you, but to also dwell within you. It is My desire to overflow your empty places with the realization of My completeness.

The thief comes only to steal and kill and destroy; I came that they may have life, and have it abundantly. **John 10:10 NASB**

Scripture Reading: John 4:1-14

*G*oing **Deeper Questions:**
1. What have you used in the past to try to fill the void and emptiness on the inside that only God can fill? How did these substitutes work for you? Were they helpful or not in helping you reach a place of fullness, peace, and contentment?

2. Water is vital to life and health. Prolonged periods without
    it leads to certain death, causing many people in third
    world countries to walk for miles for this life-sustaining
    commodity. In John 4, what does Jesus say about water?
    How would drinking from His cup daily satisfy your thirst
    and fill the void? How far are you willing to go every day to
    get the drink you need to survive?

Simple Prayer: I need You today, God, more than anything
or anyone else. Fill me with Your Holy Spirit.

Day 5
Return to the Place

*Y*our Heart's Cry

Where were You when I needed You? If You had been here, this never would have happened. If You were who You say You were, I wouldn't be going through this right now. How will I ever be able to trust You again? Where is the victory in this situation? I don't see how anything good can come from something so bad. If the Bible is true and all of Your promises within it are mine, why are they not active in my life? Why am I not seeing Your goodness in my situations? Why am I being excluded from Your table of blessings? What did I do to turn You away from me? Why did You leave me in my time of greatest need?

How long, O Lord? Will You forget me forever? How long will You hide Your face from me? How long shall I take counsel in my soul, having sorrow in my heart daily? How long will my enemy be exalted over me? Consider and hear me, O Lord my God. **Psalm 13: 1-3 NKJV**

*H*is Reply

I am here now, and I was there then. I am the beginning and the end of all that concerns you. Nothing can separate Me from you, but everything tries to separate you from Me. I am standing in the place of your every need. I am your refuge and your portion. When difficulty comes, seek Me by faith. Trust that I am for you, and not against you. Believe that I will never leave or forsake you. When all seems lost, I know the way you should go. I know the path of healing and restoration. My thoughts surpass the limitations of your understanding. I have made My home in your heart, and it is My desire to abide with you in this secret place. When you need Me, you will find Me in the place that belongs to you and Me alone. Go back to the place of your perceived abandonment. I was there. Stop looking for Me in the middle of the pain, and start looking for Me above the loss and disappointment. I am your covering. I am your shelter. I stand above every situation. I have never abandoned you, and I never will.

Every word of God is pure: he is a shield to those that put their trust in him. **Proverbs 30:5 NKJV**

Scripture Reading: John 11:17-44

*G*oing **Deeper Questions:**

1. In the story of Lazarus, Mary and Martha were disappointed Jesus had not come quickly to their aid. When in your life have you had an urgent need and it seemed as if no help was available? How did this time affect your relationship with God?

2. Psalm 13 shows that even King David had moments when he felt God had abandoned him. Where or in what life situation did your ability to trust God suffer the biggest blow? Where have you laid down your hope? Return to that place in your heart and your mind today. Open the door, and if the rock of pain covering that place is too heavy for you to lift, ask Him to roll away the stone for you.

Simple Prayer: Set my heart, mind, soul, and spirit free to trust You completely, Lord.

Day 6
Guilty as Charged

*Y*our Heart's Cry

The sins of my past lay before me like flower petals scattered along the aisle, awaiting the soft steps of the coming bride. My shame is apparent for all to see. There is no use denying who I've been and all I've done. There is no point to acting as if it never happened. It occurred, and I was a willing participant. I chose the path I would take. I picked the companions I would travel with. I followed the counsel of those who I believed would help me reach my desired destination. Somewhere along the journey, the dim view of my purpose became a black hole, and I sank deeper into the prison of my guilt. Somewhere along the way, I lost my way. Instead of looking for a way out, I settled for a place called apathy. Tethered to the shame, I bear the weight of my past, daily laboring under the pressure of a debt I cannot pay.

My guilt has overwhelmed me like a burden too heavy to bear.
Psalm 38:4 NIV

*H*is Reply

I have never asked you to carry this baggage. You claimed it on your own, but you do not have to keep it. Lay it down. I stand with extended hands, offering you a divine exchange. Will you release what is in your hand to receive what is in Mine? I am your gift of forgiveness. I am your righteousness. Lay down the weight of guilt, and pick up the gift of My redemption. Open up a door of faith to allow My mercy to rule in places where guilt once resided. Make room in your life for My unmerited favor.

Nail your guilt to the cross right now, in this moment. Receive My finished work for what it is. Every sin you've ever committed is erased. Condemnation has been replaced by acceptance. I have broken the power of guilt in your life. You are released, free to move with a lightness that testifies to your liberty. You have been freed through the power of My grace.

In my anguish I cried to the LORD, and he answered by setting me free. **Psalm 118:5 NIV**

Scripture Reading: John 8:1-11

Going Deeper Questions:

1. In Mark 2:17, Jesus compares the forgiveness of sin to the healing of disease. "It is not the healthy who need a doctor, but the sick. I have not come to call the righteous, but sinners." In what ways has the guilt of your past sins brought disease into your life?

2. Right now, write down every sin that immediately comes to your mind you are guilty of committing, either in your past or presently. Is there a common theme among these sins? Do they primarily deal with a need to feel loved, are they centered around issues with trust, or can you see a pattern of fearful thinking arising? See Jesus drawing a line in the sand. On one side stands every sin on your list; on the other side,

Jesus stands shielding you. Your accusers no longer have the power to hurt you. You are covered. You are redeemed. You are free from the bondage of your past.

Simple Prayer: Lord, reveal to me the wonder of living in Your liberty.

Day 7
Powerless to Overcome

Your Heart's Cry

The battle between the me I want to be, and the person I see has left me weak. Fatigue has paved a trail in the hardened ground of my heart. It has moved aside all peace and joy, leaving behind doubt and unbelief. Each cut to my emotions is carving out a canyon, deep and wide, dividing the landscape of my hope. Somewhere at the bottom of that canyon I sit. Weak from the heat, weary from the exertion, worried by my predicament. There is no light to help me find my way out. I've been down here so long I don't think I will ever get out. The more I try, the deeper I sink into this cavity of emotional decay. Where can I turn when I feel utterly helpless? Where will my strength come from when there is no strength to be found?

Fear not, for I am with you; be not dismayed, for I am your God; I will strengthen you, yes, I will help you, I will uphold you with my righteous right hand. **Isaiah 41:10 NKJV**

His Reply

When you are helpless, I am not. Turn towards Me in the midst of your struggles, and you will find I have already turned towards you. I am able to lead you through any trial, no matter how daunting the journey may appear. I have secured your place in My presence. Every problem you face serves to bring you closer to Me. Allow the knowledge of My love to become a banner over you. Let it be your insurance. Let it be your sanctuary. Remove the burden of self-sufficiency, and receive the security of My ability.

My ways are not your ways, so let Me lead you. It is sometimes necessary for Me to avoid taking you through the shortest route to My desired end. The journey is where our relationship is built. It is in the day-to-day process of living that you begin to see Me for who I am. I am the One who saves, delivers, and redeems. Journey with Me into a deeper understanding that I am your help when you feel helpless.

The Lord your God in your midst, the Mighty One, will save; He will rejoice over you with gladness, He will quiet you with His love, He will rejoice over you with singing. **Zephaniah 3:17 NKJV**

Scripture Reading: Exodus 13:17-22

*G*oing **Deeper Questions:**

1. In Exodus 13, we see God moving both by day and by night. Just because things get dark does not mean it's time to stop in your tracks and set up camp in the middle of the darkness. In what dark moments have you found yourself mentally encamped?

2. Taking the long route may not be the quickest way between two points, but sometimes it can be the best way. What character traits (or fruits) can be developed when you are led through the wilderness instead of being led around it? (see Galatians 5:22).

Simple Prayer: Lead me out of the wilderness, Lord, and into a place of fullness.

Day 8
At Arm's Length

Your Heart's Cry

At times, I just want to escape. Move beyond the difficulty. Sidestep the heartache. Leap over the obstacles. Sometimes I wish I could just run away from it all. Leave behind the cares of this world and jog into a reality that is currently just a fantasy. Somewhere out there, just beyond my reach, await possibilities and opportunities, sitting arm's-length away. Close enough I can feel it, yet far enough away to leave me wanting. If I try harder, do better, or be more, maybe just maybe I can stretch out mid-stride and grasp the prize before me. So I keep running and running, sometimes toward and sometimes away.

You were running a good race. Who cut in on you to keep you from obeying the truth? **Galatians 5:7 NIV**

His Reply

Running is only healthy if it leads you to a place of strength. Let your running take you back to the beginning. In the beginning was the Word, and I am the Living Word. Don't run away from life. Running away from life is the same as running away from Me. Instead of running, slow down and walk toward an understanding of who you are in Me. You are a child of the Most High. Your future is clothed in My promises. My foundation of love and truth are the track on which you can explore the plans I have for you. Make a move towards unwrapping your life from the confines of your control. Take one step out on hope, and another step out on grace. I know those who are Mine, and you are Mine. Can a mother forget her nursing child? Neither can I forget you. Walk daily this new path of relationship, and it will lead you back home to My heart.

Therefore, since we are surrounded by such a great cloud of witnesses, let us throw off everything that hinders and the sin that so easily entangles. And let us run with perseverance the race marked out for us. **Hebrews 12:1 NIV**

Scripture Reading: Luke 15:11-24

*G*oing **Deeper Questions:**

1. In the story of the prodigal son, the son is eager to run away from what he has known in search of something better. In what ways can you relate to the son in the story?

2. What is the father's reaction when he sees the son approaching? What do you think God's reaction is each day when you set aside time to come to Him?

Simple Prayer: *Draw me after You and let us run together!*
Song of Soloman 1:4 NASB

Day 9
Love's Sacrifice

Your Heart's Cry

I cannot feel love. I've looked in the arms of a lover, but the love I craved was not there. All I found was a door to more shame, a reflection of my own pain. I've tasted the hint of love's honey upon my lips, words spoken silently to the wounded places in my heart, only to be left unfulfilled when the promises were never kept. What I thought was love then showed its true character. Love has failed to reveal to me its purpose in my life. I'm at the end of myself. I've got nothing lovely left to offer. All of the fight inside of me has died. I'm drowning in my discontent, stuck in the valley of the shadow of death. Love is dead to me, and I am dead to love.

Even though I walk through the valley of the shadow of death, I will fear no evil, for you are with me; your rod and your staff, they comfort me. **Psalm 23:4 NASB**

His Reply

I am love, and I am not dead. The love inside of you is a seed. This seed has potential and power, yet its greatest power is found in burial. When a seed dies and falls to the ground, it appears all is lost, but, in reality, it is not dead. It is hidden for a season to allow time for maturity and growth. The type of love that is able to withstand the test of time can only be formed in sacrifice. Love pays a price. I am love, and I paid the price for you to live daily. Stop looking for love externally and look internally. My love springs forth from the inside. It germinates in the deepest part of your heart and bursts through the hardened ground. When you are at the end of yourself, you are touching the hem of Love's sacrifice. Love is patient. It hopes, and it believes, even when up against great odds. Love's purpose is to ignite growth and sustain life. Love's ultimate purpose was fulfilled on the cross. Love is not dead. Love is alive.

We have come to know and have believed the love which God has for us. God is love, and the one who abides in love abides in God, and God abides in him. **1 John 4:16 NASB**

Scripture Reading: Luke 23:26-36

*G*oing **Deeper Questions:**

1. Love is the foundation of life. When you feel distant from love, the desire to obtain it can lead you into counterfeit love relationships. How has craving love affected your relationship with God and others?

2. To abide means to dwell or remain in a place. To abide in love is to remain in a place of confident knowledge that you are loved by God. Even when you are in a difficult situation, abiding in love reminds you of Whose you are. In Luke 23, what ways did Jesus continue to abide in love? What benefits are now available to you because of Love's sacrifice on the cross?

Simple Prayer to: Teach me how to abide in love, Lord.

Day 10
Held

*Y*our Heart's Cry

Pulling and pulling, I wrestle to free myself from what surrounds me, moving away from the gravitational pull of today's emotions. Holding my breath, I attempt to keep the pain from squeezing through the tiny cracks in my façade. Maybe today will be different. Maybe today it won't hurt so bad. Maybe today the numbness will overcome the pain. Maybe today won't be like every other day. When will it all stop? When will the difficult cease being difficult? When will the impossible become possible? How long can I continue my current course? How much more can I endure? If I continue wrestling, will I eventually get to a place of freedom?

Come to me, all you who are weary and burdened, and I will give you rest. Take my yoke upon you and learn from me, for I am gentle and humble in heart, and you will find rest for your souls.
Matthew 11:28 NIV

*H*is Reply

Stop struggling and enter into My rest. The fight you sense inside of you is the fight over to whom or to what will you surrender your cares. The stress of self-sufficiency is constricting, slowly tightening with each attempt to be the lord over your own life. It is not good for you to be held captive by anything. Money, fear, illness, nor sorrow can ever draw you so deep into the trappings of this life that I do not have the power to pull you out. No one and nothing can snatch you out of My hands. You are held, as secure within My embrace as your level of surrender. The more you surrender to Me, the easier you are to hold. Stop struggling and let Me carry you to the new place I have prepared for you.

Humble yourselves, therefore, under God's mighty hand, that he may lift you up in due time. Cast all your anxiety on him because he cares for you. **1 Peter 5:6-7 NIV**

Scripture Reading: Hebrews 4: 9-11

*G*oing **Deeper Questions:**

1. In Hebrews 4, those who refuse to set aside a time of rest ultimately find themselves perishing. How is omitting rest harmful to your well-being?

2. Surrendering your cares, your anxieties, and your worries are part of the process of resting in God. What do you need to surrender today?

Simple Prayer: Lead me in a path of sweet surrender, Lord.

Relationship With Others

Day 11
Marriage Matters

Your Heart's Cry

There is a stranger in my bed. Coming and going, in and out of the shadows of my life. Conversation is clipped. Friendship is strained. Passion has faltered. I cannot find the road back to what once was. My partner for life has become my partner in death. Daily dying in a loveless valley. Side by side, we walk together through life, but no longer joined heart to heart. Meals are shared at a table of confusion. Love is shared under a role of obligation, penetrating barely the surface of a passion that once burned hot. Made to complete each other, striving instead to compete with each other. Bound by one tiny ring on an insignificant finger. Bound by a vow I no longer know if I want to honor.

For this reason a man shall leave his father and his mother, and be joined to his wife; and they shall become one flesh. **Genesis 2:24 NASB**

His Reply

I am the passion you have lost in your marriage. How have I loved you? With patience, forgiveness, kindness, and compassion, I have pursued you. With joy, I take you daily under My wing. With persistent faithfulness, I provide for you. Now do the same. Love your spouse with the same love with which you have been loved. Pledge to know each other as friend, companion, confidant, and lover. Resist the battle for position in your home. I am the Head of your family. Once you submit to that position, everything else falls into place.

Take time to fix what has been broken. Revisit the reasons you married. What I join together is made to last, but that does not mean there will not be tests and trials. Remember you are both on the same side. Fight fair and fight together against a common enemy. You are not each other's enemy. Remember who the fight is against. Take up your position side by side and fight the good fight. Loving well is a battle position, trusting freely is another, and forgiveness is a position of great power. Your marriage matters to Me because you matter to Me.

Two are better than one because they have a good return for their labor. **Ecclesiastes 4:9 NASB**

Scripture: Ephesians 5:22-33

Going Deeper Questions:

1. Marriage is a complex exchange of needs and wants between two people who desire to love and honor the other. God's plan for marriage requires trusting not only God but also your partner. Wives, do you find submitting to your husband difficult or easy? Why? How is submitting to your husband part of trusting God's plan for your marriage?

2. Christ is the ultimate example of selfless love and devotion. Husbands, what does it mean to love your wife as Christ loves the church? How does this level of love lead to greater respect and trust?

Simple Prayer: Today I choose to renew my wedding vows.

Day 12
Twisted Hunger

*Y*our Heart's Cry

The one I married is not the one I desire. Images fill my mind of bodies and faces I'm not supposed to want. I desire what I cannot have, and it's affecting what I do have. Smiles and kind words to members of the opposite sex have gone further than I expected. What started out as flirtation has turned into intimacy. I've given more than I set out to give. I've gone further than I set out to go. There is no way back. I cannot return down the road I came. The bridges have been burned. The trust has been severed.

Life has taken the strands of my desires and twisted one need upon the other. My hunger has been interwoven with my insecurity, braided together with my fears. I want what I should not have. I desire what is not mine to desire. What good is hoping against hope for reconciliation while my needs go unmet? What consolation is there in denying the hunger my spouse refused to acknowledge? I hungered, but I was not being fed. My need to be understood, respected, and treasured was left unmet, as was my need to be needed. I found it all in the arms of another.

Be alert and of sober mind. Your enemy the devil prowls around like a roaring lion looking for someone to devour. **1 Peter 5:8 NIV**

*H*is Reply

You merely found the crouching lion waiting to devour what was precious. Every moment your attention is pulled away from what is true, is focused on a lie. The truth is, your spouse could never fulfill all your needs and neither can the one you are with now. You have twisted the focus of your hunger away from what can truly satisfy your needs. Lust is an imitation of love. It has some of the benefits of love without the commitment that makes love meaningful. Loving forever is a choice. It is a daily choice to mend bridges before you travel too far to return.

Bridge the gap your hunger has created in your marriage. First, admit your part. Your spouse is not the cause of your hunger and cannot be held responsible for your transgression. Own your actions and come to Me with a repentant heart. Confess your actions to the one you have vowed to love, and ask for their forgiveness. When they act out in pain, realize you caused that pain and allow time for the sting of the injury to lessen. Seek out godly counsel to guide your journey back to each other. Come before Me separately for individual healing then together for covenantal healing. I alone have the power to close the mouth of the lion and speak life into your relationship once again.

Submit therefore to God. Resist the devil and he will flee from you. **James 4:7 NASB**

Scripture: Proverbs 5

Going Deeper Questions:

1. In Proverbs 5, King Solomon gives words of wisdom to his sons regarding adultery. How is chasing after passion outside of the marriage bed "giving your best strength to others"?

2. Passion, when focused in the right direction, can ignite the fires of purpose and promise within your home. How would pursuing your spouse with all your strength affect the quality of your relationship?

Simple Prayer: Lord, breathe new life into my marriage.

Day 13
Leftover Love

Your Heart's Cry

Don't judge me because I sleep around. I know some think it's not right, but I'm tired of waiting for "ever after." I'm OK with sharing for a season. I'm old enough to know love doesn't last, and marriage is just the precursor to divorce. So why wait? What is the purpose of wasting my single years in obscurity? Why should I date with self-imposed limitations? My bed is big enough for two, so why not find someone to share it with? Who are you to judge me? If I'm not sleeping with your spouse then there shouldn't be a problem. I love being loved so what's so bad about that?

Turn my eyes away from worthless things; preserve my life according to your word. **Psalm 119:37 NIV**

His Reply

Love is free for you to give and receive, but intimacy is something to be valued. Intimacy allows someone into a place few should have the privilege of peeking into. The more people you let in, the less treasured this place becomes. You are a treasure worth preserving. Do you undermine your worth for momentary pleasure? Purity is not a punishment; purity is an investment. It is an investment in something of great value. It is an investment in yourself.

Ruth found her Boaz, but she had to be willing to go by way of waiting, trial, and testing. This is not to discourage you, but are in place to equip you with the character and attitude needed to enter covenant with another. Seek Me with the intensity with which you currently seek your lovers. I am the Lover of your soul, and My love is never abusive, tainted, or leftover. My love is pure and specifically for you.

So flee youthful passions and pursue righteousness, faith, love, and peace, along with those who call on the Lord from a pure heart. **2 Timothy 2:22 ESV**

Scripture: Titus 2:11-14

*G*oing Deep Questions:

1. The temptation for closeness is great. We all crave to feel loved and desired, but only God's love can truly satisfy. How can the grace of God help you to live in sexual purity before marriage?

2. There is a time of preparation and a season for all things. Embracing the current moment opens the door for your next season. In what ways can your time of singleness be a blessing of greater intimacy with Christ?

Simple Prayer: Lord, help me pursue holiness.

Day 14
Who's Pulling Your Strings?

Your Heart's Cry

When did I give away the power to control me? When did I hand over the reins of my emotions? How did I lose myself and my identity in another's vision, in someone else's dream? I long to know who I am and what I am here for. Has my time here lived up to Your expectations? Right now, I don't know what is expected of me. I've lost control. Arms and legs flail around like a puppet on a string. My only hope is that the puppet master will be merciful. Free me from the daily pull against my will and my emotions. Release me from the tug of war upon my peace. With every shift in my day, I feel the strings being pulled, jerking me back to the reality of my instability.

Such a person is double-minded and unstable in all they do.
James 1:8 NIV

His Reply

Be genuine. There is only one of you. You are an original, and there is no one like you. You cannot be replaced, for you are unique and precious to Me. Refuse to be molded and categorized into a stereotypical box. You must be free to be who you are. This world would have you conform to its image, but resist the pressure to be shaped by those around you for the purpose of acceptance. Break out of the mold and only be conformed spiritually into My image. Maintain your individuality, get real, and be content with who you are. Your authenticity is one of My many good gifts.

Circumstances and people can only control you if you give them permission to do so. To whom or what have you relinquished control? Identify what is controlling your day, and you will identify an idol that needs to come down. Your direction is led by your thoughts and your actions. So, think on those things that will lead you toward freedom. Think on whatever is true, lovely, honorable, and praiseworthy. I came not to control you, but to free you from the bondage of this life. I am no puppet master. I am your freedom and your liberty. You are not My puppet; you are My beloved. I do not control, but I will lead you if you will trust and follow Me.

The mind of man plans his way, But the Lord directs his steps. **Proverbs 16:9 ESV**

Scripture: 1 Samuel 24:1-22

*G*oing **Deeper Questions:**

1. David does not respond to Saul's behavior as one would expect. What does David's action say about who he has chosen to follow?

2. You cannot control the actions of others, but you can control how you respond to their actions. How does freedom from being controlled by people's actions release you into God's good plan for your life?

Simple Prayer: When I don't know which way to turn, I choose to follow You Lord.

Day 15
The Enemy Within

𝒴our Heart's Cry

It's never my turn. I'm tired of sitting on the sidelines watching others live the life I wish I had. How long must I be left behind, waiting and wanting? Patience has worn a hole in my resolve to be patient. Hate and hurt rise up every time I see someone else get what I feel I deserve. I will not celebrate or congratulate another who is holding what I cannot obtain. Red flows like paint down my face when I hear of each blessing I'm not getting. My internal clock ticks loudly, reminding me of wasted time and unmet expectations. So I wait, impatiently tapping my fingers on the timeline of my life. Waiting for my chance, waiting for my opportunity.

For we ourselves were once foolish, disobedient, led astray, slaves to various passions and pleasures, passing our days in malice and envy, hated by others and hating one another. **Titus 3:3 ESV**

𝒽is Reply

Get up from this place of envy and move your attention to a place of gratitude. Focusing on anyone other than Me will always lead you down a deceptive road. Focus your attention first on Me as the Giver of all good things. From every relationship, to every circumstance, this is your first position for victorious living. Next, focus on what you see Me doing. Follow Me through the pages of scripture and see what I spent My time doing. Your waiting has left you frustrated because you are waiting on an invitation that has already been extended. The envy you feel is the residue of a heart held back. The jealousy you've encountered is a sign of the limits you've placed on My ability. My supply is limitless. I am abundance, and I came so that you could live an abundant life. Once you trust in this one truth, you'll be free from the enemy within.

A sound heart is life to the body, But envy is rottenness to the bones. **Proverbs 14:30 NKJV**

Scripture: James 3:13-18

*G*oing Deeper Questions:

1. You are too unique for comparisons. God is not in the business of creating carbon copy lives. How can looking with longing at another's life lead to confusion in your life?

2. Whatever you focus on becomes largest and most prominent in your life. How does moving from envy to gratitude put you in a better position for blessings?

Simple Prayer: Lord, when I feel the sting of envy, remind me to look to You as my unlimited portion.

Day 16
Prisoner of Hate

Your Heart's Cry

I don't like your kind. It's people like you who cause all the problems. If it were not for you people, the world would be a better place. There is no need for differences. I see no goal in tolerance. If I tolerate you, I compromise me. If I accept you, I reject me. I refuse to like you, and I will not change my position on this issue. No one soils a white garment then flaunts the stain in the middle of a color parade. No one opens the door for the enemy to walk right on in. My hate is my banner. My disdain is my membership card to uprightness. I am right, and I do not care if you approve of my disapproval.

If anyone says, "I love God," and hates his brother, he is a liar; for he who does not love his brother whom he has seen cannot love God whom he has not seen. **1 John 4:20 ESV**

His Reply

If love has limits, it is not love. If hate has no boundaries, it is not merely hate but spiritual decay to your soul. It erodes your joy and your peace. You are designed to hate the evil, not the person. How can you hate your brother who you see and love Me who you have not seen. I created you both in My image. Neither is blameless or without fault. If I can accept you with your imperfection, why would you not do likewise with your brother? You do not have to agree to love. You do not have to condone to love. Love is an action worthy of active participation. Hate is a cancer designed to eat away at you internally. I have set before you life and death. Choose life and live in harmony with others.

And above all these put on love, which binds everything together in perfect harmony. **Colossians 3:14 ESV**

Scripture: Acts 10:1-33

*G*oing **Deeper Questions:**
1. It is common to judge others by your own personal standards. Right or wrong, we sometimes see those different than us as outcasts. What does this passage of scripture imply about this practice?
2. Our uniqueness is a tapestry of the creative nature of God, yet we all share in a universal experience. How does acknowledging our commonality in Christ defeat judgmental behavior patterns?

Simple Prayer: Help me to love others as You do, Lord.

Day 17
Letting Go

Your Heart's Cry

They hurt me. In the dark of the deep woods behind my childhood home, they took something I did not give. I fought in darkness, and I'm still fighting. Fighting to not be a victim of my past. Fighting to not be affected by the pain of my violation. Fighting to not lose the battle in my mind. I was powerless to defend myself then, but never again. I will not allow myself to be caught with my guard down. My wall is up. It was erected each time they came for me again. Each infraction laid brick upon brick, building a wall around my heart. The pain from the physical abuse pales in comparison to the pain of the emotional aftermath. All I can say is "I survived." I cannot forgive, and I will not forget.

Strengthen the weak hands, And make firm the feeble knees. Say to those who are fearful-hearted, "Be strong, do not fear! Behold, your God will come with vengeance, With the recompense of God; He will come and save you." **Isaiah 35:3-4 NKJV**

His Reply

Forgiveness is not about blessing those who hurt you. Forgiveness is about healing the wounds inside of you. Each painful memory you hold onto holds onto you. Unforgiveness is tethered to your life. It holds you down and holds you back from forward movement. It anchors you into the moment and keeps you prisoner to the emotional pain. The wall you erected not only keeps others out, it keeps you in. It is not enough to simply survive. Survival is the lowest form of freedom. I came so you could experience abundant life, life to the fullest extent. Free from the pain of the past and loosed from the confinements pain has created. Forgetting is not what is required, but I do ask you to turn it over to Me. Allow Me to be judge and jury over those who have hurt you. Release them to Me. Release the pain and disappointment. Release the fear and the anxiety. Release your right for revenge. Let it go into My hands.

The LORD works righteousness and justice for all who are oppressed. **Psalm 103:6 ESV**

Scripture: Mark 11:25

*G*oing **Deeper Questions:**

1. This scripture is further displayed within the Lord's Prayer "Forgive us our trespasses as we forgive those who trespass against us." Why do you think Jesus included this in His example of how we should pray?

2. Forgiveness is not a gift we give to the offender, but one we give to ourselves. How is forgiveness actually more about you than it is about the other person?

Simple Prayer: Lord, show me how to forgive those who hurt me.

Day 18
Influencers

𝒴our Heart's Cry

I am affected by the decisions of others. What I see them do drives my choices and directs my course. At times, their decisions have led me to a place I didn't want to go, but I followed anyway. My desire to be part of the in-crowd has robbed me of personal choice. I'm influenced by their judgment. I have let them make up my mind for me. I've lost my individuality in my desire to be accepted. My desire to please them is now displeasing to me. I want the freedom to choose my own course, but I want them to continue to let me into their circle even when I don't follow their lead. Can I be me and still be a part of the clique? Is it possible to not blend in and still be in without being left out?

Do not be misled: "Bad company corrupts good character."
1 Corinthians 15:33 NIV

𝓗is Reply

Long before you recognized your need to be accepted, I accepted you. I chose you in the middle of all that held you captive, because I have already seen you walking free. Free from the chains of the need to please others. Free from the bondage of performance. There is freedom in living for the applause of nail-scarred hands. There is freedom in living in the center of My will for your life. Seek Me for the answers. Seek Me when you need guidance along life's path. It is My desire to see you free. You always have a choice with Me. Blessings or cursings, life or death—it's always your choice. Choose the path that leads you closer to Me and not the one which leads you to a place of emotional distress and confusion. My path is the one that will be well lit with the light of eternal love.

See what great love the Father has lavished on us, that we should be called children of God! And that is what we are! The reason the world does not know us is that it did not know him. **1 John 3:1 NIV**

Scripture: Ephesians 1:3-14

Going Deeper Questions:
1. Trying to please everyone can cause you to miss the opportunity to please the One. How has being a people pleaser affected your identity and personal choices?
2. Acceptance is a prevailing need we all share. It feels good to know you belong and are loved just as you are. What comfort is there in knowing you have been accepted in Christ, adopted by a Holy God?

Simple Prayer: Focus my desire on pleasing You alone, God.

Day 19
The Fellowship of the Beloved

*Y*our Heart's Cry

I see no purpose in church attendance. What benefit is there for me to sit in a pew on Sunday with people I only see once a week? If God is everywhere, why do I need church? I can worship in the privacy of my home. I can pray in solitude to an audience of One. Church is simply a building of pious people flaunting their holiness. It's a group of like-minded elitists congratulating each other on having made it in. Religion is not synonymous with having a relationship with God. I'm secure in my relationship with the Almighty. The church is powerless to change me and powerless to change society. I love God, but God is not church, and God is not in most of the churches I've attended.

Worthy are you, our Lord and God, to receive glory and honor and power, for you created all things, and by your will they existed and were created. **Revelation 4:11 ESV**

*H*is Reply

The body of believers you have described is not My church. My church is built upon a sound foundation. My church is established in the atoning Blood of Christ. My church is not a lukewarm exchange of platitudes and gratitudes. My church is a fellowship of the beloved. My church is a group of believers drawn by My presence and by My Word. My church is joined together as one for one common goal: to bring glory to My

Name. My church has a purpose, and each gathering is a team-building experience. Edifying each other is part of the weekly exchange, as are correction and empowering. Relationships are at the foundation of each disciple's growth. Corporate times of praise and worship are a gift to be enjoyed, a freedom to be expressed. My church has the same power within it that raised Christ from the grave. If the place of your congregation does not fit My definition, stop calling it My church. Go find a church where My people are thriving spiritually, binding the broken-hearted, feeding the hungry and setting the captives free because this is the outward evidence of My church.

Draw near to God, and he will draw near to you. **James 4:8 ESV**

Scripture: Matthew 18:19-20

*G*oing **Deeper Questions:**
1. Church is about community. These times of gathering are for your benefit as individuals and as a body. What promise does this scripture hold for a group of believers?
2. Poverty, sex trafficking, and homelessness can seem like insurmountable problems, but by joining together, we can amplify our effectiveness in these areas. What power does the promise in Matthew 18 hold for those who can come together in unity?

Simple Prayer: Reveal my place in Your church, Lord.

Day 20
Passionate Compassion

𝒴our Heart's Cry

Sitting at the intersection, wrapped in a blanket with your dog by your side, I see you. Sign in your hand and down on your luck, I see. I see the lines on your face. I see the hopelessness in your eyes. Too proud to beg, yet too desperate to not beg. I see you, but I do not stop. I close my windows and lock my doors. I pretend I don't see, but I see you. I excuse my action or lack thereof by the many shortcomings on your part that may have placed you in your current situation. Drunkard, gambler, druggie, deadbeat—which are you? I'm not obligated to help you, and I resent the implication that you are my responsibility. Could it be possible you were once just like me, living day-to-day and paycheck to paycheck? Could it be life simply sent you a curve that set you whirling into this new place, sitting at the intersection? Could it be you are a purposeful part of my day, sent to reveal to me what I'm not seeing?

I know that the LORD will maintain the cause of the afflicted, and will execute justice for the needy. **Psalm 140:12 ESV**

ℋis Reply

Your role in this life is not to judge others, but to love others and to do it well. Loving well takes practice on imperfect recipients. See people through My eyes of love and acceptance. Accept them for where they are and love them through their current difficulty. Be gracious in your dealings with the less fortunate, for tests and hard times are a common denominator for all. Share from a place of abundance. Be My hands in a world in need of My touch. Be a reservoir of My grace and compassion.

What do you have in your hands? Are you willing to use it for another? One meal at a time. One kind word at a time. One drink of water at a time. One smile at a time. One provision at a time. One life at a time. Hope can spring forth from one act of passionate compassion. Be a living hope ambassador.

I the LORD search the heart and examine the mind, to reward each person according to their conduct, according to what their deeds deserve. **Jeremiah 17:10 NIV**

Scripture: James 2:2-8

*G*oing **Deeper Questions:**

1. Everyone is your neighbor. From the clerk at your local grocery store to the man sleeping on a park bench, you are surrounded by opportunities to love. What does "love your neighbor as you love yourself" mean to you?

2. What can you offer the next time you see someone in need? Consider filling a gallon size zip-lock bag with samples of toiletries, granola bars, beef jerky, and a bottle of water to keep in your car. Be prepared to be a blessing to another.

Simple Prayer: Lord, show me today's love assignment.

Negative Emotions

Day 21
Enemies of the Heart

*Y*our Heart's Cry

More is never enough. I crave and crave, trying to fill up the void. The more I put in, the emptier I feel. I find myself running after my passions only to end up flat on my face. I am reaching with all my strength towards things that are pleasing to the eye and easy to obtain, yet never satisfy. I deserve better. I don't want to struggle to be filled. I don't want it to be hard. I'm too tired to spend so much time in the hunt for completion. I'm not happy where I'm at, but I don't have the energy to continue striving. So I sit on my bed of discontentment. I sit and wait for something to change. Day in and day out, I go around the same emotional merry-go-round, expecting a different outcome, but I end up in the same place—unhappy and unfulfilled.

Anxiety in the heart of man causes depression, But a good word makes it glad. **Proverbs 12:25 NKJV**

*H*is Reply

Come walk with Me. Let us move away from the place of your need and into the place of your desires. What is it your heart truly desires? Your hunger will never be filled by the natural desires of this world. Fulfilling the desires of your flesh and satisfying the desires of your eyes can only bring a fleeting level of satisfaction. And with that momentary satisfaction you gain little to no lasting benefit. It is My desire for you to flee from the passion warring for your soul. It was never what your heart truly desired anyway. The longing you have is one for right relationship with Me. The deep craving of your soul is for an inner peace that is rooted in acceptance of a love you cannot fully understand. Rooted in My life-giving love for you grows the tree of righteousness. The enemies of your heart would love nothing more than for you to continue in the place you currently find yourself. I agree "You do deserve better." That is the reason why I came.

But I will sing of your strength, in the morning I will sing of your love; for you are my fortress, my refuge in times of trouble. **Psalm 59:16 NIV**

Scripture: Mark 6:30-44

Going Deeper Questions:

1. Sometimes we have to break away from the hustle and bustle to be able to hear the voice of God. Why do you believe Jesus, in the passage above, called His disciples away with Him to a quiet place?

2. Hunger is a sensation that when left unattended can lead to desperation. What does the story of Jesus feeding the 5000 say about His ability to feed your hunger?

Simple Prayer: Fill me, Lord and satisfy my hunger.

Day 22
When Panic Attacks

*Y*our Heart's Cry

Pounding, louder and louder, the thud in my chest escalates to an erratic pace. Beads of perspiration dot my forehead. Warmth spreads throughout my body, leaving my hands moist. White-knuckled fists open and close in silent protest to the war raging inside of me. I cannot control it. When panic attacks, I'm helpless to the onslaught of what-ifs closing in on me. My proposed danger is as real to me as the air I breathe. A nightly news report, I live out in the flesh. To some, these emotions are just a false reality, but for me they are a real possibility. Panic resides in me. Even in sleep, these thoughts refuse to release me. To whom can I confide the reality of my anxieties?

My beloved spoke, and said to me: "Rise up, my love, my fair one, And come away. **Song of Solomon 2:10 NKJV**

*H*is Reply

I want you to be free of all anxiety. Cast your cares upon Me. Release yourself from the intimidation that comes through uncertain circumstances. Take captive each thought attempting to capture you. Be done with the worry that nags at your heart and causes anxiety. Fix your mind on what is true, right, pure, and lovely. Think about things that are excellent and worthy of praise. You are fully equipped to fight back against this attack, but in My strength, not yours. Resist the temptation to rely on your own strength. Allow Me to lead you into truth and victory. Receive the help I offer. Receive the help of those I use to stand with you against this enemy of the soul. Be at peace. Do not be anxious. Give Me the proper priority in your life and trust Me with the details.

Do not be anxious about anything, but in everything by prayer and supplication with thanksgiving let your requests be made known to God. **Philippians 4:6 ESV**

Scripture: Hebrews 3:7-19

Going Deeper Questions:

1. In Hebrews 3, we hear of the rest the Israelites forfeited because they refused to listen to God. How does taking time to listen to God help produce rest for His people?

2. Every negative emotion has a goal: to pull you away from the truth of God's Word. How does anxiety accomplish this, and what tools can you use to fight back the next time it attacks?

Simple Prayer: Calm my anxious mind, Lord.

Day 23
Feel the Fear

*Y*our Heart's Cry

I look within for the strength to move forward, but the strength is not there. All pretense of self-sufficiency has dissolved in the river of much uncertainty. The currents of my fear propel a flowing cascade away from what I desire, but toward all that torments me. Night rages on in silent distress as my body refuses to release its hold on me. My mind refuses to release the anticipation of things that could be, things that may never be, and things that currently only exist in my head. Yet, it all appears so real. I see into the darkness all that lies in wait for me. Where can I go when the darkness gets darker? When all I feel is fear, how do I find my way back to faith?

The Lord is my light and my salvation; whom shall I fear? The Lord is the stronghold of my life; of whom shall I be afraid? **Psalm 27:1 NIV**

*H*is Reply

Fear is a spirit, but it is not from Me. Fear waits in the recesses of your imagination, seeking an opportunity to appear real. Fear leads to an emotional state of dis*ease*. It creates a reciprocal response empowered by how you react to what is beyond your control. Fear was never meant to be a dwelling place; it is only a point along the journey of life. It's an abyss determined to keep you immobilized in your perceived place of safety.

When fear threatens you, hear My voice calling you to launch out into the deep with Me. Hear the whisper of My promises in the midst of it all. Be courageous and fear not. I am greater than your biggest fear, and I will be with you all the way. I have given you My very best to overcome the spirit of fear, and you are not powerless. You have been given the spirit of power, love, and a sound mind. With the help of My spirit, you will rise above fear's negative pull. Stay grounded in My love for you and know you have the power within you to do all I have placed in your heart to do. Remember, fear does not know you as well as I know you. You are an overcomer.

For God has not given us a spirit of fear, but of power and of love and of a sound mind. **2 Timothy 1:7 NKJV**

Scripture: Mark 4:35-41

Going Deeper Questions:

1. In the scripture above, a group of skilled fishermen are terrified by a coming storm. Isn't it interesting, the thing that frightened them so greatly was something their life revolved around: the sea? In what areas of your life are you tempted to respond with fear rather than faith?

2. What can we learn about how Jesus feels concerning our fear from this story?

Simple Prayer: Speak peace to my fears, Lord.

Day 24
Silent Sorrow

𝒴our **Heart's Cry**

I remember the night death came. You were not there. You were not there when my loved one inhaled a final breath. You didn't see the sorrow that framed the moment. You didn't hear the internal screams escaping from a place I didn't know existed. The news slammed into my happy life with the finality of a gunshot. Deep pain oozed from my soul and dripped upon the landscape of my forever. Day and night merged into one long reminder of the loss, the wounding, the injury to my heart. I wept in silence. I was too stunned to respond, too scared to react. I endured the graveside service, tear-stained and shoulders weighted. In that casket lay my expectations of the future, when it slammed shut, so did my will to feel again.

Blessed are those who mourn, for they shall be comforted. **Matthew 5:4 NKJV**

ℋis **Reply**

Your sorrow is not without voice. I am touched by your grief. I have seen your tears, and I have heard your heart's cry. Each tear is precious to Me. Not a single one has gone unnoticed. I have collected them all. Before I came, death was your final enemy. But I have overcome death and the grave. All who believe in Me will have eternal life. Death has no victory. It's victory has been defeated by the joy of My promised return. I am faithful

to keep every promise. In your moments of pain and loss, weep. I too have felt the sting of this pain, and I understand. But do not reside in this place of sorrow forever. In everything, there is a season. Take My hand and allow Me to lead you out of this valley of the shadow of death. Allow Me to move you through this winter season back into a place of springing forth with renewed joy. You will sing with gladness once again.

Weeping may endure for a night, But joy comes in the morning. **Psalm 30:5 NKJV**

Scripture: John 11:1-45

*G*oing **Deeper Questions:**

1. In this passage of scripture, we are shown how Jesus deals with loss. His reaction to the death of his friend Lazarus is the shortest, but one of the most comforting scriptures in the Bible. "Jesus wept." How does it make you feel, knowing Jesus knows how you feel in times of sorrow?

2. Not every prayer is answered as we hope. Sometimes God's purpose does not line up with our desires. But even in these times, His intentions are always to reveal to you the wonder of His grace. In the story, Martha was very disappointed Jesus did not arrive before Lazarus died. Why do you believe Jesus waited before coming?

Simple Prayer: Lord, just hold me while I weep.

Day 25
Beyond Anger

*Y*our Heart's Cry

The spasm of my jaw muscles and the furrowing of my brow are the small outward workings of the anger I hold inside. The strain of the daily grind and the inability to adequately unwind has brought me to the edge of despair. Fury rages, boiling underneath in the surface of my calm and collected guise, awaiting the tiniest infraction upon my well-planned schedule. Hand hard upon the horn, blaring my displeasure at incompetent drivers. Harsh words exchanged with the receptionist who failed to meet my needs. Curses spoken over my kids and spouse for not meeting my unrealistic expectations. Anger defines me, and I am powerless to control its pull on my emotions.

But you, O Lord, are a God merciful and gracious, slow to anger and abounding in steadfast love and faithfulness. **Psalm 86:15 ESV**

*H*is Reply

From where does this anger arise? Anger in itself is not a problem. It is misguided anger that leads to death and destruction, not only for the one who is angry, but for those who are hurt as a result of that anger. Your anger does not arise from a place of righteousness. Your anger is coming from a place of emptiness. With a bitter heart, you have lashed out with your tongue and used your words like a whip to beat those around you. Controlling your anger is possible when you allow yourself to feel the internal pain you are trying to escape and deal with its root issues. Resist the temptation to dilute your pain by inflicting pain on others. This will never satisfy and will only perpetuate the cycle of pain in which you currently live. Let Me show you a better way to release the pain you harbor inside.

Know this, my beloved brothers: let every person be quick to hear, slow to speak, slow to anger; for the anger of man does not produce the righteousness of God. **James 1:19-20 ESV**

Scripture: John 2:13-16

Going Deeper Questions:

1. Flipping tables and driving people out of the temple with a whip can certainly be viewed as an angry outburst. Yet scriptures let us know Jesus lived a sinless life. What do you feel is the difference between His anger and yours?

2. What have been the results of your anger at home and are these the results you desire? Proverbs 19:11 states "Good sense makes one slow to anger, and it is His glory to overlook an offense." How can applying this principle improve your relationships?

Simple Prayer: Cleanse my heart, Lord, and reveal any unrighteous anger.

Day 26
Breaking the Cycle

*Y*our Heart's Cry

I see you following the same path I've taken. Following close on the heels of my past failures. The sins of the father have been passed down to the son. The iniquities of the mother are the dowry of the daughter. The cycle continues: poverty, alcoholism, obesity, depression, fear. Each cycle is held by a root of torment, deep within our generational line. With every child born, our prayer is that the cycle will be broken, and the chains of this bondage will be loosed. Yet, here we remain, bound and yearning to be free. Circling once again, as new birth brings in another generation of the enslaved and downtrodden.

The LORD your God is with you, the Mighty Warrior who saves. He will take great delight in you; in his love he will no longer rebuke you, but will rejoice over you with singing. **Zephaniah 3:17 NIV**

*H*is Reply

Every captive shall be set free through the acceptance of the finished work of the cross. Sin has reigned for too long within your household. This cycle of self-destructive behavior is long past its termination date. Begin by determining what is at the core of this cycle. Repent of your part in the behaviors that keep this cycle alive. Next, stop battling with your weapons and exchange them for Mine. The fight for your freedom is not with flesh and blood, but with powers and principalities. You will only be successful when you draw on My power and not your own. Lastly, align your will with My will and align your words with My words. Resist falling back into the cycle again, and use the power of your tongue to speak blessings over your future.

Death and life are in the power of the tongue. **Proverbs 18:21 NKJV**

Scripture: Ephesians 6:10-18

*G*oing **Deeper Questions:**

1. Ask any military personnel, and they will tell you the most important parts of warfare are having the right equipment and a strategy to defeat your enemy. God has given us His best to equip us, but we must daily choose to put on His armor. What armor do you need to put on today?

2. What will your strategy be next time the temptation arises to repeat past negative cycles in your life?

Simple Prayer: Break every generational chain of bondage in my family line, Lord.

Day 27
Shame Interrupted

*Y*our Heart's Cry

I don't deserve Your love. You don't know what all I've done. You don't know who I've been. If you knew, the disapproval on Your face would be evident for all to see. I've stood in places no one should stand. I've participated in actions that can only be described as mistakes. One wrong choice after another with no exit door for the shame I hold inside. I carry the blame for my shame. My choices led me down this road, and it is these choices that have held me bound. I find myself running away from You. I cannot bear for You to see me like this. So, I come before You veiled, covered by layers of regret. I am not worthy of Your love.

I sought the Lord, and he answered me and delivered me from all my fears. Those who look to him are radiant, and their faces shall never be ashamed. **Psalm 34:4-5 ESV**

*H*is Reply

My love is not for sale. It cannot be purchased, nor can it be earned. My love simply is. It is yours for the taking. I know all you have done, and I still love you. Look deeply and you will see not eyes of disapproval, but eyes of love and compassion. A wrong choice is just one choice away from being right. Choose to be free from the bondage of your shame. Do not let the shame, nor the sin allow you to continue in the same cycles, for they have become obstacles and hindrances in moving forward. I have

come to interrupt the power of shame in your life. For too long, shame has been the dividing line between us. No more. Shame has lost its control over you. You are free to stand boldly before Me. Trust Me to love you—all of you—even when you do not love yourself. I alone can make you whole and set you free.

If we confess our sins, He is faithful and just to forgive us our sins and to cleanse us from all unrighteousness. **1 John 1:9 ESV**

Scripture: Hebrews 10:1-10

Going Deeper Questions:

1. In the Old Testament, sins were only forgiven by the shedding of the blood of animals. Every year a sacrifice would be made to cover sins. How is Christ the ultimate sacrifice?

2. Is there any sin bigger than the cross? No. How does knowing this truth move us from shame and guilt to repentance and righteousness in Christ?

Simple Prayer: I surrender my shame and receive Your righteousness, Lord.

Day 28
No More Hiding

*Y*our Heart's Cry

Life goes on, unaware of my existence. Would anyone know if I just ceased to be? Would anyone care if my journey ended? I fear my time on the Earth has been without event, without fanfare, without meaning. Did I accomplish anything of lasting value? Did I do what I was sent here to do? I sense I have not. I do not feel I have reached high enough or gone far enough in my pursuit of significance. My failures stack up around me like little piles of manure, leaving the foul smell of my past in the middle of my small successes. I cannot compete. I cannot compare. I feel too small to be a sufficient influence because the pain of my insecurity is too big for me to ignore.

In a desert land he found him, in a barren and howling waste. He shielded him and cared for him; he guarded him as the apple of his eye. **Deuteronomy 32:10 ESV**

*H*is Reply

Who said you were small? Resist the temptation to compare and judge based on your understanding. Know My ways are much higher than your ways, and My thoughts are higher than your thoughts. Your view of failure is not My view. What you see as displays of your weakness, I see as growth opportunities. The smallness you feel is only in your thoughts. I did not create you to be small. I created you to be a beacon of light penetrating the darkness. Your significance can only be established in Me and My plan for your life.

No more hiding in the shadows of your own insecurities. No more hiding behind the faulty belief that you are insignificant. For, what man puts a lamp under a blanket? Neither have I placed you in hiding. You are positioned for glory. You are positioned to shine right where you are. No one can compete for your place, and no one can compare to being you. It is you who I desire to live your life, and no one can do a better job at it than you.

I will give you hidden treasures, riches stored in secret places, so that you may know that I am the LORD, the God of Israel, who summons you by name. **Isaiah 45:3 NIV**

Scripture: Genesis 1:26-27

Going Deeper Questions:
1. God made you in His image. What does that say about how He feels toward you?
2. In the scripture above, God gives us the responsibility of ruling over the Earth and displays a lot of trust in His creation. Why does God not fear our failures?

Simple Prayer: God, give me a confident heart to overcome my insecurities.

Day 29
Scars

Your Heart's Cry

I've been marred in the Potter's hands. The wounds went deep, cutting into places no one sees and leaving me forever marked. Damaged goods. The physical wounds you can see pale in comparison to the hidden ones I carry in my soul. The framework is there, but there is no substance in this temple. A fragile and weakened vessel of disgrace. If only you could peek inside. Then, you would be able to adequately determine the degree of my injuries. Then, maybe something could be done to heal the hurt.

Heal me, O LORD, and I will be healed; save me and I will be saved, for you are the one I praise. **Jeremiah 17:14 NIV**

His Reply

I see your scars, and I will not turn from them. Your scars are valuable to Me. They do not repulse Me, but rather draw Me closer to you. Each one of your scars is beautiful and unique. Each one carries a memory of a time I have touched you and healed you. The wounds you still carry are ones you have not released to My healing touch. Your physical body does not war against healing. It is designed to always move towards health and wellness, even through risk of pain and discomfort in the process. Your physical wounds are much easier to heal than those you carry in your spirit. Your emotional wounds can only be healed when you are ready to give Me full control of the process. These wounds are the ones that will become your testimony. These are the wounds that will proclaim my faithfulness and bring Me glory. These wounds came with a cost and carried a high price for your healing. I willingly paid that price. See, I have scars too.

And after you have suffered a little while, the God of all grace, who has called you to his eternal glory in Christ, will himself restore, confirm, strengthen, and establish you. **1 Peter 5:10 ESV**

Scripture: John 20:24-29

Going Deeper Questions:

1. Scars are a part of the healing process. What scars (physical or emotional) do you possess that are reminders of past difficulties? How can these scars be a reminder of times God has healed and restored?

2. When Jesus returned to show Himself to the disciples, He came with His scars. He could have healed them, so why do you think He chose to keep His scars?

Simple Prayer: Help me see my scars as beautiful reminders of Your grace, God.

Day 30
The Dance of Pride

*Y*our Heart's Cry

I don't need God. I can make a plan and execute it without any assistance. And if plan A does not work, I always have a plan B ready. I'm at the top of my game. I am gifted at what I do. I need no one's approval to succeed. I have already defined my personal success. If God has a purpose for my life, that is His problem and not mine. I will not lower my expectations to meet Christian standards. I will not be a pauper for the gospel. I will only walk the paths I have chosen. All other paths are inferior. I am the captain of my ship and the master of my destiny. My purpose is to fulfill my dreams and live out my own expectations. Is there any greater glory?

In his pride the wicked man does not seek him; in all his thoughts there is no room for God. **Psalm 10:6 NIV**

*H*is Reply

Pride is a dance that will lead to a great fall. It must be discarded and replaced by a spirit of humility. It is My desire for you to find your confidence in Me alone. Everything else is fleeting, here today and gone tomorrow. It is My pleasure to care for you. Just look at the flowers in the fields. They do not labor for their needs. Their beauty is bright and abundant. They beam with a radiance that shines bright for all to see. They don't receive this glory for themselves, but point it all back to their Creator. Do likewise.

Be careful of the path you choose to walk. This path of self-reliance is one with many pitfalls and unstable ground. This path has costs you have not counted. Turn away from the destructive path of your pride and return to humility. Walk in humility, and you will find a greater level of confidence on the receiving end of My favor and grace.

But he gives more grace. Therefore it says, "God opposes the proud, but gives grace to the humble. **James 4:6 ESV**

Scripture: Genesis 3:1-13

Going Deeper Questions:

1. From the time of the fall of mankind, pride has been one of the core problems. Satan himself was consumed with his pride and was crafty enough to draw man into the same temptation. What prideful temptation did Satan use to convince Eve to taste of the forbidden fruit?

2. After giving in to temptations, Adam and Eve went from a fruitful relationship with God to one of hiding and shame. How does pride tear a rift in our relationship with our heavenly Father?

Simple Prayer: Father, give me a humble and teachable spirit.

Identity

Day 31
The End of Me

Your Heart's Cry

I have no more answers to the questions clouding my mind. I don't know which direction to turn nor do I have the desire to keep searching. Moving forward from this place requires effort, and I've reached the end of my desire to care. My heart is heavy, and my strength is waning. Any energy left is only enough to give life to my misery. How long can suffering last? Is there a time limit on hopelessness? The fire falling upon my life has reduced me to a vapor.

Make me know Your ways, O LORD; Teach me Your paths.
Psalm 25:4 NASB

His Reply

Make space for Me in your life. Where you end, I can begin. Lay aside everything causing you to feel distant from Me. Pull away from the distractors, which daily come to block you from a deeper relationship with Me. Let My Word remind you of the good future I have planned for you. Receive a fresh downpour of My presence every morning. Start each day open to receive My assistance. Do not wait until you have exhausted all of your strength. I am God at the beginning of your struggle, just as I am God at the end. I am here along the entire journey. My availability is eternal.

Every ending is also a beginning. Seek out the new thing I am doing within you. If you find yourself at a roadblock, look to Me for your next step. Take My hand and let Me guide you through. The path may be foreign to you, but it is not to Me. There is no road you can take that I have not traveled first. You are hemmed in on all sides by My love.

I am the Alpha and the Omega, the First and the Last, the Beginning and the End. **Revelation 22:13 NIV**

Scripture Reading: Ruth 1:1-21

Going Deeper Questions:
1. The book of Ruth opens with the tragic story of Naomi. In verse 21 she laments, "I went away full, but the Lord has brought me back empty." Like Naomi, do you blame God for your misfortune? How does this attitude affect your ability to follow where He leads?
2. At the end of this passage of scripture, Naomi makes the decision to return home to Bethlehem. Home is symbolic of a place of provision, safety, and comfort. How is time with God also a decision to return home?

Simple Prayer: Lead me home, back to the place of intimacy with You, God.

Day 32
Beautiful Discipline

Your Heart's Cry

I'm seeking You, but You seem so far away. Grace at a distance beckons me to run faster toward the promised peace. The legs of my faith spasm under the stress of hope deferred. Like a good soldier I try to endure, but my strength is failing, and my energy is low. My spiritual breathing is fast and erratic, no longer able to keep up with the demands of living maxed out. I am not prepared for this race. I have not adequately trained for this level of exertion. How far must I run to reach You? What emotional distance must I cross to find myself surrounded by Your love?

Brothers, I do not consider that I have made it my own. But one thing I do: forgetting what lies behind and straining forward to what lies ahead, I press on toward the goal for the prize of the upward call of God in Christ Jesus. **Philippians 3:13 ESV**

His Reply

This time of devoted togetherness is working within you a beautiful discipline. Seeking Me is a process that teaches you how to run with patience and endurance. Then, when you find Me, you are able to rest confidently and know I am God. I am God of your past, I am God of your present, and I am God of your future. Life is a continuum, moving you along a path from glory to glory. Find times of refreshing in the watering of My Word. Breathe a deep breath and receive the assistance of My spirit. Stretch your faith muscle and believe again. You are further along than you realize. Continue to run the race set before you. Your reward will be worth the effort.

Everyone who competes in the games goes into strict training. They do it to get a crown that will not last, but we do it to get a crown that will last forever. **1 Corinthians 9:25 NIV**

Scripture: Hebrews 12:1

*G*oing **Deeper Questions:**

1. Preparing for a race requires putting in the needed hours to train well. Without doing the work of training, you will be ill-prepared to run your best race. How is life similar to running a race?

2. Elite runners pack light. They have learned it's hard to run their best race when they are carrying excess baggage. What effect would being weighted down have on your race performance? What weights do you need to strip off to run more effectively?

Simple Prayer: Lord, show me what I need to lay down so I can run my best race.

Day 33
Imperfect Courage

Your Heart's Cry

Moving forward is going to take more courage than I have. I fear taking a step outside of this comfortable place I've found. I fear making a wrong move. When I look back over my life, I don't want to see failure. I don't want to risk jumping into something not equipped to support the weight of my dreams. I refuse to confront another letdown. So I wait. I wait for a sign that it's OK to proceed. I wait for permission to be me, permission to take a chance on living bold faith. It's courage I lack, yet it's courage that is required to reach the place of my longing. Therefore, I will continue to stand here in-between my past and my future. Here is not where I want to be, but the familiarity binds me.

So do not fear, for I am with you; do not be dismayed, for I am your God. I will strengthen you and help you; I will uphold you with my righteous right hand. **Isaiah 41:10 NIV**

His Reply

Courage is found in a place of trust and surrender. Cease fighting to have your way. Let go of your need to control the outcome. Rest in the knowledge of My sovereignty. Rest in the faithfulness of My goodness toward you. When you decrease, I increase. The more of Me free to live within you, the greater your courage will be. The fear you feel is the residue of those places you refuse to surrender to Me. When you surrender all you hold back, you surrender the fear.

Fear comes to impede your progress, but I have come so you may walk in liberty. I am your ever-present help. Your imperfect courage is all that is needed to succeed. Take a step towards the hope I've placed inside you. You have My permission to live a life of courageous faith. Ask Me to expand your ability to believe. Expect My favor and know it is My will for you to prosper and be in good health even as your soul prospers.

When I am afraid, I will trust in you. In God, whose word I praise, in God I trust; I will not be afraid. What can mortal man do to me? **Psalm 56:3-4 NIV**

Scripture: 1 Samuel 30:1-19

*G*oing **Deeper Questions:**
1. After losing all that was important to him, David inquired of the Lord if he should attempt to retrieve what was taken. What losses in your life do you feel the Lord has given you permission to pursue and recover?
2. Verse 6 in this passage states, "But David encouraged and strengthened himself in the Lord his God." How is this an example of being imperfectly courageous?

Simple Prayer: Lord, grant me the courage to release back into Your capable hands what I've held.

Day 34
Shattered Confidence

Your Heart's Cry

Once again, I am the loser. Failure has become my constant companion. I walk through seemingly open doors only to find barriers I did not expect. Obstacles stand in my way, taller and more ominous than ever before. How many times can you fall before you break? Time and time again, my confidence is shattered. I am nothing. My gifting is limited. I am not able to compete with those in my field. Why send another resume? Why take another risk? Why hope again? Why try again? Have I not fallen short enough times already? I refuse to ask again, seek again, or dream again for fear of yet another no.

Therefore let us draw near with confidence to the throne of grace, so that we may receive mercy and find grace to help in time of need.
Hebrews 4:16 NASB

His Reply

I am for you and not against you. The work I have started within you will be completed. I am here to take you past old boundaries and old ways of doing things. With confidence, you will proceed into the new. Rise and shine for your light has come, and My glory is shining all around you. Do not grow weary in the face of the enemy. Break through the glass ceiling of your self-confidence and receive My confidence. I came to break you through into an expansive place, a place with room for you to be authentically who I created you to be. Stretch out your stakes and enlarge your boundaries with assurance that I will go with you every step of the way.

Begin where you are, not where you desire to be. Use what you have available to you. Do an assessment of what you have in your hand. Moses had a rod, and I used it mightily. Know that every journey begins with the first step. Stumbling is part of the process. Pick yourself up and begin again. It's a new day. Let My strength rise up inside of you. Not by might, not by power, but by My spirit, you will move with renewed confidence. It's time to gather the broken pieces and dream again.

For I am confident of this very thing, that He who began a good work in you will perfect it until the day of Christ Jesus. **Philippians 1:6 NASB**

Scripture: Psalm 40:1-3

*G*oing **Deeper Questions:**

1. Time spent waiting on the Lord in expectation of His presence is always rewarded. In this scripture, God rewards David by taking him out of a pit of destruction. What pit are you currently in or have been in?

2. Confidence is a seed that requires daily watering to grow. How can a relationship with Christ build your confidence?

Simple Prayer: Restore my ability to rest in Your sufficiency, Lord.

Day 35
Painted Fences

*Y*our Heart's Cry

Look at all the pretty fences. Each lined up in a row. Every home holding in secrets no one will ever know. I sit behind the walls that have become my emotional defense. Will you peek behind the façade? Look deep inside and see the dysfunctional paradox that has become my reality. I share this not for pity, since pity has no point. I share this only to let you know, the things you envy are all just a beautiful front. There is no time for rest. No time for prayer or self-care. The constant action behind the fence is quickly taking me nowhere. I cannot find the joy that once defined my life. So I sit and stare at my neighbor's fence and wonder what's going on over there. This cannot be all there is in the life we have on earth. I do not want to waste my years painting fences behind which I die unhappy and unfulfilled.

But I have raised you up for this very purpose, that I might show you my power and that my name might be proclaimed in all the earth.
Exodus 9:16 NIV

*H*is Reply

I look beyond the fences. I look deep inside your heart. I see the dysfunction, and I see the missing parts. In all your searching for beauty and in your search for love, you failed to search for the One who looks down on you from above. Your joy can only be made complete in the seat of My mercy and grace. Your actions will only lead to purpose when you take time to rest and experience My embrace. My plan for you requires self-care, joy, and peace. Looking at your neighbor's fence will not produce what you need. Take time to look inside yourself. Reflect on what you find. Make note of what I reveal to you, and you will find this is the most meaningful use of your time. Spend daily time in My presence and walk in wellness, wholeness, and health. In this, you will find a treasure of great value and worth.

Search me, O God, and know my heart; Try me and know my anxious thoughts; And see if there be any hurtful way in me, And lead me in the everlasting way. **Psalm 139:23-24 NASB**

Scripture: Colossians 2:2-10 (read The Message Bible version)

Going Deeper Questions:

1. What benefits are available to you when your mind is confident and at rest, focused on Christ?

2. Everything in the universe is brought to a place of fullness in Christ. How does spending time in His presence help to fill the emptiness and produce a life of wholeness?

Simple Prayer: Help me to spend my time wisely and in ways that glorify You, Lord.

Day 36
Infinite Potential

Your Heart's Cry

Inadequate is the word that best defines my abilities. I am ill-prepared to accomplish all that is in my heart. I'm limited in my resources, unsure of my purpose, and uncertain of the promise. This is the barren wilderness in which my dreams wander, unfulfilled and undernourished. Starved-out and famished from a diet of fear and doubt. So I sit on the precipice of now, fixated in my current stagnation. Inspiration fails to visit, and encouragement has waved farewell long ago. The dryness in my mind has slowly dried up the hope in my heart.

But now, O LORD, You are our Father, We are the clay, and You our potter; And all of us are the work of Your hand.
Isaiah 64:8 NASB

His Reply

Creativity is at the heart of who I am. Because I am creative, you are creative. There are no limits to the potential inside of you, only limits on your ability to dream. Let Me share My dream for you. Surrender your desire to see your plan completed and trust My plan will be greater than anything you could imagine. My vision is infinite. It transcends time and all human reasoning. You can't see what I see. I know what has been deposited within you. You are capable of far more than you give yourself credit for. I am the dream giver. The dreams I give are for an appointed time and season. Just because it has not happened yet does not mean it will not ever happen. Every good work is completed at its due time. Release your desire to control the outcome and trust Me with the process. Now, come dream with Me.

I am raising you up, My beloved, with a fresh sense of purpose, direction, and destiny. My desire for you is that you would release everything from the past that would hinder your progress. I can open doors before you that no man can shut. I can bring opportunities that cannot be hindered unless you choose to step back from them. Do not be afraid. Do not hesitate. Do not hold back. Go forth in My name and by My authority. You have everything you need to walk in the fullness of your calling.

In the beginning, God created the heavens and the earth. The earth was without form and void, and darkness was over the face of the deep. And the Spirit of God was hovering over the face of the waters. **Genesis 1:1-2 ESV**

Scripture: Exodus 35:30-35 and 36:1-2

Going Deeper Questions:

1. In this passage of scripture, is God generous or stingy in His giving of talents to Bezalel? What internal giftings did he receive?

2. These gifts inside Bezalel had been there since birth, but at the appointed time, God revealed their purpose and showed Bazalel his calling. What do you believe the Bible means in Exodus 36:2 when it says, "God stirred his heart"?

Simple Prayer: Stir my heart to dream Your dream for my life, Lord.

Day 37
I Choose Whole

Your Heart's Cry

I am broken. All hope and expectation have been shattered against the hard surface of my life, now only fragments remain. Pieces fall around me and litter my mind with memories of a better time. The fragility of my emotions is evidence of the pain that still remains. The pressure of past disappointment and poor choices continues to crush my resolve. I long for joy, but joy is a complex puzzle I have yet to put together. I need to see the big picture. The broken view from where I stand is lined with stress, distress, and disease.

Make me to hear joy and gladness, Let the bones which You have broken rejoice. **Psalm 51:8 NKJV**

His Reply

I see your brokenness, and I am here to heal, but you must come to Me. Give Me the broken pieces of your life and trust Me to mend them. I cannot minister to your needs and bring life and hope from far away. I desire to heal you and make you whole in every way, but I cannot when you hold yourself away from Me. It is not enough to read My Word and to know about Me. You must come near. Come close so I may touch you, touch your heart, heal your brokenness, and satisfy your longing. Relationship with Me requires intimacy, which is not possible unless you come away with Me, My beloved.

Wholeness is My plan for you. I take what is broken and make it anew. Let me breathe a fresh wind over your emotions. Trust Me with your brokenness. Receive the grace to rest in a new and unfamiliar place of wholeness. Choose to be made whole.

Gather the pieces that are left over. Let nothing be wasted.
John 6:12 NIV

Scripture: John 5:1-11

Going Deeper Questions:
1. Sometimes you can be broken for so long, it becomes a comfortable place. Why do you think Jesus asked this man "Will thou be made whole?"
2. Change requires you to take a step into the unknown. Why does choosing to be made whole require courage?

Simple Prayer: Give me the courage to choose to be made whole, Lord.

Day 38
Purposeful Discovery

*Y*our Heart's Cry

My seeking has shown little to be excited about. I've looked in the pages of literature. I've researched psychology and inquired of the great philosophers in search of a deeper understanding of the purpose of life. Words alone do not suffice to move me toward my destiny and away from my uncertainty. My studies have only served to further confuse me. Conflicting doctrine with revolving theories echoes the chaos I'm trying to figure out. If I could see a purpose in the suffering then maybe this life would have meaning. If I can make sense of the pain, then maybe it would not seem as if this has all been a poorly played game.

All Scripture is inspired by God and profitable for teaching, for reproof, for correction, for training in righteousness; so that the man of God may be adequate, equipped for every good work.
2 Timothy 3:16-17 NASB

*H*is Reply

A way has been paved for you to discover the mysteries hidden inside you. In Me, you will find who you are and your purpose for existing. You are not here by chance. You were born with a destiny, for such a time as this. You have a divine assignment. The more you learn who I am, the clearer the view of your future will become. Choose to invest your time in discovering My character through My Word. Spend your hours researching and pondering the truths you find there. My Word is a rich treasure. Dig deep.

Do not settle for the best thing you can think of. Instead, ask of Me, and I will show you great and mighty things you know not of. Open your mind to explore and study so you may be at the cutting edge of My will and purposes. Follow closely, and you will go far.

My son, pay attention to what I say; listen closely to my words. Do not let them out of your sight, keep them within your heart; for they are life to those who find them and health to a man's whole body. **Proverbs 4:20-22 NIV**

Scripture: Isaiah 30:15

Going Deeper Questions:

1. Strength can sometimes be found in the most unlikely places. Where does Isaiah 30:15 say strength can be found?

2. The mysteries of life are unfolded in the pages of the Bible. Returning to the Word and resting in the truth is a formula for self-discovery. How can time spent in God's Word help you understand your identity and life purpose?

Simple Prayer: Lord, reveal to me my purpose.

Day 39
Good Enough for Now

Your Heart's Cry

Most Christians I know are holier than holy. They don't sin, and they don't hang with those who do. They have their act all together. They are not like me. I mess up, and I mess up often. When I clean up my act, I'll come to You. I am not worthy to come closer in my current condition. Too many obstacles stand between us. The blemishes on my record are countless. I want to do better, but better takes more self-control than I currently possess. The bad in me comes to the surface more than the good. I'm not good enough to be in Your presence.

For I do not do the good I want, but the evil I do not want is what I keep on doing. **Romans 7:19 ESV**

His Reply

Beloved, I want to bring you to a position of security in Me. I accept you just as you are. This mindset is one that must be destroyed, because it is a lie. There is nothing you need to change for Me to receive you. I welcome you to simply come. I am waiting for you to come boldly. I am not asking you to reach a level of perfection before you proceed. I am calling you to start on the path I've placed before you and keep moving forward. Get past the fear and the mindsets that are trying to stop you from advancing. Access has been granted. I give you permission to proceed. Meet Me in this embrace. I am your Lover, your

Savior, and your Friend. I love you just as you are, but I love you too much to leave you as you are. Do not concern yourself with those who would judge you. I alone am the judge of sin. I have weighed your sin against the redeeming work of the cross, and I judge you forgiven and accepted.

Be strong and courageous, do not be afraid or tremble at them, for the LORD your God is the one who goes with you. He will not fail you or forsake you. **Deuteronomy 31:6 NASB**

Scripture: Luke 15:11-32

*G*oing **Deeper Questions:**

1. It's comforting to know that even when we are at our worst, the Father welcomes us home. Verse 20 is the pivotal turning point saying, "He arose and came to his father." This is a faith choice we each must make in our lowest moments. What emotions do you believe the son felt when he made this decision? How would the son have expected the father to respond to his past poor choices and his current decision to come home?

2. Now, look at this passage from the position of the father. How is the father's response one of love and not judgment?

Simple Prayer: Father, give me the faith to come to You even when I feel unworthy.

Day 40
Mirror Image

Your Heart's Cry

Do you see me? Can you peer behind the walls around my heart at the places I hide inside. Do you like what you see? The real me isn't pretty. The real me is flawed and imperfect. The real me is ugly on many levels. The real me must stay hidden behind your preconceived image of me. The real me must remain tucked away safely behind the gates of your filtered vision. Is there any wonder why I tire in the midst of this award-winning performance of being who you want me to be? If only I could just be the real me.

I praise you, for I am fearfully and wonderfully made. Wonderful are your works; my soul knows it very well. My frame was not hidden from you, when I was being made in secret, intricately woven in the depths of the earth. **Psalm 139:14-15 ESV**

His Reply

I do not see what you see. All that would separate us, every sin and every pain is cast as far as the East is from the West. When I look at you, I see the light of love, the promise of peace, the hope of joy, and the one whose pain was never meant to be a wall. You are not flawed. You are filled with the beauty of My sacrifice. You are a reflection of My great love. Come to Me just as you are. Lay down your mask and step out from behind your walls. Let Me see the real you, the you I already see.

The uneasiness you feel is the pain of transitioning into the person I know is within you. Transition produces an uncomfortable sense of instability, as the comfort of familiarity is shaken by the change that is imminent, yet hard to define. You are vulnerable in this state. Like a caterpillar, you must find a safe place to reside while I complete the work I'm doing inside you. Hide yourself in Me, and let Me reveal to you the beauty of what you are becoming.

As far as the East is from the West, so far does he remove our transgressions from us. **Psalm 103:12 ESV**

Scripture: Genesis 16

Going Deeper Questions:

1. In Genesis 16, Hagar is running away from a painful place. How are hiding behind a façade and running similar coping mechanisms?

2. Have you ever encountered "The God Who Sees Me" along your painful path? If so, how did it make you feel, knowing you were not alone? If not, take a moment right now to ask Jesus to show you what He sees when He looks at you.

Simple Prayer: Reveal to me what You see, Lord, when You look at me.

Changes

Day 41
The Breaking Point

*Y*our Heart's Cry

I'm so tired. I lay down at night, tossing and turning as thoughts of tomorrow fill my mind. Tomorrow. Tomorrow is simply a reminder that once again, I will be behind and fail to complete all I have planned. My daily to-do list never ends. Each day begins in a time deficit. I am a slave to my work, and it's a hard taskmaster. I am stretched to the breaking point. I can't take another day of living stressed-out, burned-out, and worn-out. I'm pulled in every direction, except for the one I desire to go. This isn't living; it's a slow death.

The Sabbath was made for man, not man for the Sabbath.
Mark 2:27 ESV

*H*is Reply

I love giving you good gifts. But gifts are only useful if you choose to receive them. Rest is one of My good gifts. Yet, in your need to accomplish more and become more, you have set this gift up on a shelf. You view it as a gift for later, one to be used when you have the time. My rest is not a gift to be saved, but one to be continually used. It cannot be exhausted. There is an unlimited supply. In rest, you will find what you need to become flexible and pliable again. Rest is the key to not breaking under the pressures of this life. Rest takes you to a place of knowing Me better. Sit and feel the wind going to and fro, know the magnitude of My power. Breathe in the fragrance of the blossoms as you stroll down your streets, know the peace I give freely. Taste the sweetness of fruit in its season, know I am good. In all your planning, you omitted the one element that enables you to live fully: rest.

Be still, and know that I am God. **Psalm 46:10 ESV**

Scripture: Genesis 2:2-3

Going Deeper Questions:

1. Since all scripture is beneficial for growth and edification, why do you think the Bible made a point of emphasizing that God rested on the seventh day?

2. If the God of the universe took a rest, what does that say about your personal need to rest? Are you observing a personal time of purposeful rest weekly? If not, why? And is your reason worth your sanity?

Simple Prayer: I release my days to You, Lord, as You show me how to rest.

Day 42
Downsized

*Y*our Heart's Cry

I didn't deserve to be laid off. I did the work. I put in the time. I was a good employee, but it was not enough. Why did I get downsized while others still have a job? Was I not good enough? Was I not smart enough? What put me on the chopping block? How am I going to pay the bills? How am I going to care for my family? They don't deserve this either. It's not fair. Life is not fair. Where do I go from here? I'm too old to learn something new and too young to retire. So many questions fill my mind, none of which I can answer. And while I search for answers, the past-due bills continue to come with no resources for funding and no hope of getting caught up.

But you, O LORD, are a shield about me, my glory, and the lifter of my head. **Psalms 3:3 ESV**

*H*is Reply

I know you feel wounded by the actions of others, but their actions do not limit My ability to bless your life. You are not your job, your profession, your degrees, or your titles. You are Mine, loved and held in high regard. It is My good pleasure to open up new doors of opportunities. It is My will to use every event in your life to take you from glory to glory. Use this time to do an internal inventory of the gifts I have placed inside of you. Use this time to search My Word for guidance and direction.

There is more available to you than you currently can see. Trust Me and trust that this will work out for your ultimate good. I alone can see your yesterdays, todays, and tomorrows. I know how to move you forward into the future you have hoped for.

"For I know the plans I have for you," declares the Lord, "plans to prosper you and not to harm you, plans to give you hope and a future." **Jeremiah 29:11 NIV**

Scripture: Proverbs 3:5-6

Going Deeper Questions:

1. Trusting God can be difficult when events do not line up with your plans. How does leaning on your own understanding position you for disappointment? In what ways are faith and trust intertwined?

2. Acknowledging God includes seeking His Word and guidance about all that concerns you. Spend time today reading His Word. Write down the scriptures that spoke to you personally. Now place these scriptures someplace where you can see them frequently today so they can remind you of His presence and His promises.

Simple Prayer: Trusting You, Lord, to provide for our needs.

Day 43
Tailor Made For This

*Y*our Heart's Cry

I'm the sock with no match to make a pair. I'm the black sheep who does not fit in with the rest of the family. I'm the single gray hair on a 30 something-year-old's head. I simply don't belong. I don't belong with the saints, and I don't belong with the sinners. I don't adhere to the mold everyone desires to put me in. The deeds of my past leave me suspended in mid-air, hung by the nails of sorrow and regret. My mistakes have stacked up and hemmed me in on all sides. I find no reason to continue striving to conform to a life I do not fit in.

Godly sorrow brings repentance that leads to salvation and leaves no regret, but worldly sorrow brings death. **2 Corinthians 7:10 NIV**

*H*is Reply

Beloved, do not become mired in regret for things that might have been or could have been that were not. Refuse to allow the hopelessness and sorrow that follow regret to gain a stronghold in your life. What seems like a sense of loneliness, of not belonging, and of being out of sync is really a deep yearning for intimacy with Me. Don't be distracted by trying to find fulfillment through activities or relationships with others. Let your desires propel you into My presence. Refuse to allow these feelings to drive you into isolation. Do not translate this feeling into rejection. Shake off this spirit of heaviness that has settled on you like a garment.

Press in. Seek Me with a whole heart. Do not continue to gaze upon Me from afar; enter in and see Me face to face. Let go of all fear and insecurity. Allow Me to cleanse your heart, for My desire is to have you abide in My presence. I am a God of love, and I will not turn you away. I long to have you close to Me. I am doing that work in this season of your life. I am drawing you to Myself in a new way. Be sensitive to My voice as I call you to a closer walk with Me. Quiet your soul and move towards Me with purpose and determination. You were made to reside in My presence.

You will seek me and find me, when you seek me with all your heart. **Jeremiah 29:13 ESV**

Scripture: John 18:15–27

Going Deeper Questions:
1. Peter had vowed to Jesus that he would rather die than deny Him. However, in this passage, he denied Him three times. How do you think Peter felt at the end of this ordeal?
2. Despite any emotions of shame or regret, Peter was able to press past these obstacles and go on to become one of the fathers of the early church. His understanding of the person and work of Christ overcame his emotions and any feelings of failure. What regrets do you need to move past today?

Simple Prayer: I bring to You my regrets and accept Your invitation to press in, Lord.

Day 44
The Parent Trap

*Y*our Heart's Cry

I wish I never had children. The constant noise and the persistent bickering have worn down my patience and shattered my nerves. I can't take any more. Their laughter provokes me to shouting. Their playing leaves our home a hopeless mess, thus more shouting and more stress. The good times together are eclipsed by the daily struggles of parenthood. Trapped in an 18 year sentence with people I love, but cannot tolerate.

Behold, children are a heritage from the Lord, the fruit of the womb a reward. Like arrows in the hand of a warrior are the children of one's youth. Blessed is the man who fills his quiver with them!
Psalm 127:3-5 ESV

*H*is Reply

Children are a blessing from Me. They are arrows awaiting direction and launching. Resist seeing them as an inconvenience or as a chore. They are blessings, but even blessings come with responsibility. Children cannot survive apart from parental care. Release your need to make them more like you and let them be a reflection of Me. Let them be a reflection of living free. You have lost your understanding of freedom. You have lost your understanding of joy. Let the teacher once again become the student. Come to Me like a little child, recognizing your inability to survive spiritually without Me. Let your children lead you back to Me. Find joy through the eyes of a child. See life from their position of freedom. Learn once again how to play, rest, and love with liberty. Let your children show you the way out of the trap you are in.

All your children shall be taught by the Lord, and great shall be the peace of your children. **Isaiah 54:13 ESV**

Scripture: Matthew 18:1-4

Going Deeper Questions:

1. The free-spirited nature of children can be difficult to appreciate as an adult. What can we learn from children about freedom and liberty?
2. In Matthew 18, Jesus says we must become like a child to enter the kingdom of Heaven. What do you believe His statement means? What is 'childlike faith'?

Simple Prayer: Jesus, set me free to laugh and play once again.

Day 45
Cutting it Close

*Y*our **Heart's Cry**

I feel it all slipping away. The firm roots I have planted are being pulled up. The foliage of my life is slowly being clipped away. Day by day, I feel barer and more exposed. A mound of change piles up around me, fuel for the fire that I feel is to come. I cannot bear to see it all go up in smoke. Where favor once lived, destruction has come. Where blessings once resided, cursing has moved in. When did the tables turn? Where did I fall from grace? Did I make You angry, God? The slope on which I'm slipping is taking me further away from the joy I once experienced in my salvation.

Restore to me the joy of your salvation, and uphold me with a willing spirit. **Psalm 51:12 ESV**

*H*is **Reply**

I am well pleased with you. In your time of favor and blessings, you grew in knowledge and wisdom. Your heart was turned towards My will and My plan. Your tongue was that of the learned, speaking encouragement and peace over all you've encountered. Do not allow this season to change who you are in Me. This season has not come to take away from you, but to enlarge and equip you. There is more I have for you. To receive the abundance of My plans for your future, you must be strong enough to bear the weight of the blessings to come. You are in My hand, and it is My will that you grow according to My specifications. If you will yield to the process of cultivation, I will prune and refine you spiritually, so you represent Me in every aspect. Rejoice in your time of pruning. It is at this time I am closest to you as I carefully inspect and cut away only those things needed for your growth. I am right by your side to uphold and keep you.

Surely God is my help; the Lord is the one who sustains me. **Psalm 54:4 NIV**

Scripture: John 15:1-5

Going Deeper Questions:

1. Pruning is not a sign of God's displeasure but rather a sign of His enlarged vision for your life. What areas of your life have you experienced a season of pruning? What did you feel during these times? Did it seem like a promotion or a punishment? How can a right perspective change your thoughts about pruning?

2. Pruning can be a painful process. No one enjoys the feeling of loss, but the end result of pruning is always worth the pain endured. What steps can you take during the pruning process to encourage yourself? How will abiding in Christ help preserve you during times of great change?

Simple Prayer: Cut away what is needed for my growth, Lord.

Day 46
Stepping Up

*Y*our Heart's Cry

Everything that can be shaken is shaking. Changes are occurring so quickly that I hardly have the time to register one transition before another starts. My life is moving at an accelerated pace, and I no longer have the ability to slow down this progression. I was comfortable in the familiar bed of my habitual routine. This new thing You're doing in my life is perceived, but not welcomed. I want to return to the times when life was stable and things stayed the same. I want to return to the times when faith was not required, because nothing was at risk. This new season frightens me.

Now faith is the substance of things hoped for, the evidence of things not seen. **Hebrews 11:1 NKJV**

*H*is Reply

There are no comfort zones in this world. It is My desire for you to never become stagnant, always moving from glory to glory. My goodness is available to you, and My blessings are waiting for you. Leave the past behind, along with those things that have hindered you, like fear, anger, grumbling, and complaining. A season of adjustment is upon you, but you will have to mentally and emotionally let go of things that tie you to the past before you can move forward. If you will take this step of faith, you will come into a place of liberty and fulfillment you have not known before. Trust Me to bring you through this awkward transition with great grace. All you have to do is be willing and flexible.

Come up into a new place of faith. You receive what you have the faith to believe. Elevate your capacity to believe and you elevate your capacity to receive. Come higher. Place your focus on Me and not your problems. Choose worship over worry. Make a decision to desire the fullness of the blessings I have laid up for you. Bless others freely. You will find the more you pour out into the lives of others, the more I pour into your own life.

But without faith it is impossible to please Him, for he who comes to God must believe that He is, and that He is a rewarder of those who diligently seek Him. **Hebrews 11:6 ESV**

Scripture: 1 Chronicles 4:9-10

Going Deeper Questions:

1. Isn't it wonderful you are not your name or any names anyone may have labeled you with in the past. Jabez was so named by his mother because of the pain she experienced during labor. What names placed on you by yourself or by others have you believed about yourself?

2. Jabez prayed with bold faith. He stepped outside of his comfort zone and cried out to God with a great request. He asked God to bless him greatly, expand his sphere of

influence, and give him opportunities to be a blessing. But he didn't stop there. He also asked God to guide him, so the future blessings to come would not cause harm to himself or others. Do you believe God wants to bless you? How is the prayer of Jabez an unselfish request?

Simple Prayer: Bless me so I can be a blessing, God.

Day 47
Golden

𝒴our Heart's Cry

I do not know when I became old. I did not see it coming. Every year was a year closer to my grave date, but each year I still felt the same. Then, eventually, things started to change. My eyesight dimmed. My joints have started to ache and crack when I move. My weekly visit with friends became monthly visits to the doctor as friends died one by one. I do not recognize this old person staring back at me in the mirror. I no longer feel I have any value. I no longer feel I am of any use to anyone. I do not want to be a burden to my kids and family. Tonight, as I lay down to sleep, I'll pray the Lord my soul He'll keep. I'll pray I die before I wake, then the Lord my soul He'll take.

Do not cast me off in the time of old age; forsake me not when my strength is spent. **Psalm 71:9 ESV**

𝓗is Reply

Life is a gift. Each day is an opportunity. Long life is a blessing, not a curse. When you feel your strength is gone, lean on Me. Rely on the source of your strength. Come to Me for clarification of your purpose in every season of life. I am redefining your boundaries in order to make very clear to you the parameters of your responsibilities at this stage of your life. As the Ancient of Days, I will show you the hidden treasures of My word and bring you into alignment with My will. Allow Me to dwell in your midst, walk with you, and talk with you. As you do, it will not be difficult to walk by faith.

With time lived has come wisdom that was unobtainable in your youth. Teach the next generation. Guide them in My truths and help them to overcome by the word of your testimony. Meet with Me in the battlefield of effectual fervent prayer. Pray out of your current understanding for your children and grandchildren. Pray with the heart of one who has already been places those coming after you are only now just entering. You are needed, so occupy your time well.

Even to your old age and gray hairs I am he, I am he who will sustain you. I have made you and I will carry you; I will sustain you and I will rescue you. **Isaiah 46:4 NIV**

Scripture: Psalm 91:9-16

*G*oing **Deeper Questions:**

1. Psalm 91 is filled with promises of God. What are seven promises you find for those who love God?

2. Long life is one of the blessings of God. If you are still breathing air, then you are still a part of God's plan. Is there anything God has prompted you to do during these 50 days? Time is precious and not promised to anyone. Make time today to do what He has spoken to you.

Simple Prayer: Show me how to order my days, Lord.

Day 48
The Way Home

Your Heart's Cry

Home. I know somewhere a place exists where my heart can sit quietly in the comfortable armchair of life and recline into the soft contours of contentment and peace. Somewhere sits a fire lit by the heat of my past mistakes and fanned by the purity of a grace I've yet to fully grasp. Somewhere out there is the road that will lead me back to a place I left so long ago that I can no longer tell if it truly existed or if it was only a childhood illusion.

The Spirit and the bride say, "Come!" And let the one who hears say, "Come!" Let the one who is thirsty come; and let the one who wishes take the free gift of the water of life. **Revelation 22:17 NIV**

His Reply

Beloved, it's time to awake. Your walk with Me is like a nearly forgotten dream. Your heart has been divided. You have lost your way. But, I say to you, come home. I wait for you with open arms and a heart of compassion. Leave behind the things that do not represent Me and My love for you. Be done with your search for satisfaction in the things of the world, for your life is hidden in Me.

I have gone before you to prepare a place for you. Direct your gaze in My direction and take a step of faith towards Me. I am your resting place. I am the pathway to your peace. I am the door into all hope. Seek Me and you will find Me, when you seek

Me with your whole heart. There is always room for you at My banquet table. I have prepared this table for you in the presence of your enemies. At this table is a seat with your name on it, a seat where all of your past adversaries will see you seated in My redemptive grace. Take your seat. Feast on My promises. Feast on My truths. Welcome home, My beloved.

And God raised us up with Christ and seated us with him in the heavenly realms in Christ Jesus. **Ephesians 2:6 NIV**

Scripture: John 14:1-6

Going Deeper Questions:

1. What do you think of when you hear the word home? What feelings and emotions do you relate to home? How do your thoughts of home compare to the image of home Jesus offers?

2. In this scripture, Thomas asks Jesus "How do we know the way to where You are going?" In His reply, Jesus reveals where our true home resides. How is life in Christ home?

Simple Prayer: Show me the road back home, Jesus.

Day 49
Growing in the Dark

Your Heart's Cry

The darkness is closing in around me. It engulfs all I know and obscures my ability to see past this moment. Zero visibility. No vision. No plan. I grope into nothingness, hoping to find something of worth, but my hands return empty. Every step is an act of faith. Movement is constrained and I often find myself at a full stop. Fixated in the dark. Grounded by my hemmed-in perception.

Where there is no prophetic vision the people cast off restraint, but blessed is he who keeps the law. **Proverbs 29:18 ESV**

His Reply

Do not fear the darkness. I am not in the darkness, but I can use darkness to display the power of light. I am the Light of the world. In Me is no darkness. Let Me show you the darkness inside so it can be released, and light can come in. Things that have been hidden in the dark recesses of your heart will be brought to the light where you can see the truth. The radiance of My glory shines out to dispel the darkness. Take My light into the dark places. Allow the illumination to show you what you have not been seeing. Eyes that have become used to darkness must be refocused to see in the light. Change your perception. Every good fruitful seed spends time in the dark. This is the place where growth happens. This is the place where new beginnings sprout and the past is dispelled. Continue to reach up toward Me. I will strengthen you in the process. I will reveal to you My plan for advancement. I will supply all you need as you stretch beyond where you are now to where you desire to be.

And my God shall supply all your need according to His riches in glory by Christ Jesus. **Philippians 4:19 NKJV**

Scripture: 2 Samuel 22:17-31

Going Deeper Questions:

1. This scripture is part of a song David sang after God delivered him from the hands of his enemies. Enemies can be anything or anyone with a goal to harm you, including people, situations, emotions, and addictions. What enemies have been attacking you in the dark places of life?

2. Verse 29 compares the Lord to being a lamp. How is having a lamp helpful when you walk in darkness? How is light the ideal weapon against darkness?

Simple Prayer: Enlighten my darkness and light my way, Lord.

Day 50
Shifting Sands

Your Heart's Cry

The sands of time are quickly moving past me, shifting my focus and my resolve. I am running out of time to finish all I have planned. Ten years seemed adequate to accomplish my goals, yet they have still not manifested, and this is year number twelve. I fear starting over. I fear embracing a new dream, so I continue with the one that has failed to work. I continue to work my plan. I continue to push and prod against the goads. Time has not been kind, and I am offended by its resistance to accommodate my timeline, my desires, and my will.

So teach us to number our days that we may get a heart of wisdom.
Psalm 90:12 ESV

His Reply

It is good to have a vision and to have a plan, but resist being bound to it. Resist the temptation to be overwhelmed with your responsibilities. Refuse to allow your emotional reactions to get you off course. Move ahead with courage and assurance that I am with you. Open your hands. Hold loosely the days before you. Offer your plans to Me and receive My plan, My vision, and My purpose for your life. You cannot walk the path or live out the days before you get there. You must live today to the fullest and allow Me to fill you with truth and wisdom that will bring clarity and perspective. Refuse to allow fear to rule your hearts and minds. Sit quietly, watch carefully, and wait patiently, for time will reveal My plans and purposes. Be pliable and resilient. It is not too late. Time has not passed you by. Each day is an opportunity, a gift of the present. I am the door to your second chance. I am the way, the truth, and the life. Allow Me to re-order your steps and re-form your path.

The heart of man plans his way, but the Lord establishes his steps. **Proverbs 16:9 ESV**

Scripture: Ephesians 5:15-20

*G*oing **Deeper Questions:**

1. In this passage of scripture, we learn time can be redeemed. Merriam-Webster Dictionary defines "redeem" as a verb, meaning to make better, to exchange, or to buy back. What does the phrase "redeeming the time" mean to you?

2. Wisdom is available to all who ask God for it. We are to walk in wisdom so we will be able to understand God's will for us. What role does wisdom play in redeeming the time?

Simple Prayer: Please order my steps, Lord.

Illness

Day 51
Under the Knife

*Y*our Heart's Cry

I'm scared. The cold hard stretcher presses hard against my back. The white crisp hospital sheets spread across my body. I'm surrounded by masked covered faces, staring down at me. The eyes behind the mask appear tired and drained. My confidence fades. I need this surgery, but a stream of "what ifs" fill my thoughts. What if I have a reaction to the anesthesia? What if the doctor messes up? What if something goes wrong and I don't wake up? What if …? My mind drifts slowly away from this place. The medication begins to slowly claim my consciousness. My fears are numbed, even if only for the moment. I know they will return later.

May you be strengthened with all power, according to his glorious might, for all endurance and patience with joy. **Colossians 1:11 ESV**

*H*is Reply

When you are presented with a situation out of your control, know I am still in control. When you are at your weakest, I am at My strongest. I am not changed by your circumstances or the events in your life. When everything else seems to be falling away, I remain. My strength is made perfect in weakness. There is nothing too hard for Me. Even your doctors and nurses are in My hands. Trust Me to see you through every difficult situation.

I am as close as the air you breathe. Release a silent prayer of expectant thanksgiving. Expect all things to work together for your good.

And we know that God causes all things to work together for good to those who love God, to those who are called according to His purpose. **Romans 8:28 NASB**

Scripture: Romans 5:1–5

Going Deeper Questions:

1. It is very difficult to consider rejoicing during times of suffering, but in these verses we are shown how God can even redeem those difficult times. What are some potential good fruits that can come out of a season of suffering?

2. Verse 5 in this passage states, "Hope does not disappoint." In what way is hope the best medicine of all?

Simple Prayer: May tests and trials never steal my hope in You, Lord.

Day 52
Ribbons in the Sky

*Y*our Heart's Cry

You did not ask my permission to come. Like a thief, you came in the dark of night and took what you wanted. You took my peace, you took my joy, you took my security, and you took my health. The biopsy results still echo in my heart "Cancer." It wasn't the hair loss, the nausea, the vomiting, or the weight loss I hated. What I hated most was the fear you brought with you. It's been years since the surgery, and I still wake up in a panic, dreaming I've found a new mass. Every ache is magnified out of proportion. Every change is deemed the worst until proven otherwise. You did this to me. You came unannounced and crushed my happy life.

Praise be to the God and Father of our Lord Jesus Christ, the Father of compassion and the God of all comfort.
2 Corinthians 1:3 NIV

*H*is Reply

Even cancer cannot overcome the victory of the cross. The love I have for you is stronger than the fear you've faced. Fear has to do with a thought that you are being punished. I am not punishing you. I am not upset with you. Although this cancer is not of Me, I will use it for My glory. My love towards you is stronger than any cells in your body. My love is all-consuming. You have not had to take one step of this battle alone. During the

biopsy and surgery, I was there. Through every chemotherapy, I was there. I was your companion at every doctor appointment and your pillow on which you cried yourself to sleep those many nights. I was not absent in your time of need. I was there, standing in the gap between the pain you were experiencing and the future joy to come. I was there, keeping a record of all you were enduring and planning your path to overcome.

There is no fear in love, but perfect love casts out fear. For fear has to do with punishment, and whoever fears has not been perfected in love. **1 John 4:18 ESV**

Scripture: Isaiah 61:3-4

Going Deeper Questions:
1. Every trial can be redeemed. In Isaiah, we are told we will receive beauty for ashes. What does this phrase mean to you? Have there been times it feels like life has burned you? What joy can be found in knowing beauty can arise from those ashes?
2. No matter where you are geographically, God expects us all to bloom where we are planted. When a flower blooms, it reveals its beauty, not to testify about itself, but rather about the God who created it, nurtured it, and clothed it with splendor. Blooming is a result of yielding to the Creator. He does the work while you rest in Him. How do times of illness help us learn how to rest in Him?

Simple Prayer: Raise beauty from these ashes, Lord.

Day 53
Forgotten Mercies

*Y*our Heart's Cry

Today is not one of my good days. Today I can't recall Your name. Your face looks familiar to me, but the years have caused me to lose track of time. Sometimes I fear I will forget my own name. Every day, as I head out of my house to walk the familiar neighborhood, I wonder if I will remember how to get back home. Strangers greet me, hug me, and reminisce about things I know nothing about. People visit me and hold my hand as if I mean something to them. I am so confused. I can still see memories from long ago: my wedding day and the birth of my children are as real to me now as they were then. But, who are these young ones now calling me grandma? I feel like I've lost my mind with no road map on how to get it back.

In my distress I called upon the Lord; to my God I cried for help. From his temple he heard my voice, and my cry to him reached his ears. **Psalm 18:6 ESV**

*H*is Reply

When you find it difficult to focus on all that is around you, focus on Me alone. I will be your constant in the confusion of your mind. I will be the foundation on which you can find a place of stability. Cling to the memories of the past and take each day as it comes. Receive love from those who offer it. Know My mercies are new every morning. With each day, I give fresh grace.   Rest your mind. When the questions rage and there appear to be no answers to the confusion you feel inside, enter into My presence and enjoy the peace you will find there.

But I trust in you, O LORD; I say, "You are my God." **Psalm 31:14 ESV**

Scripture: 1 Peter 1:3-9

Going Deeper Questions:
1. Dementia is a disease that not only affects the person living with it, but all those who love them. Although names and faces may be forgotten, there is living hope in Jesus. Through Him, we have an inheritance in heaven. What adjectives are used to describe this inheritance in verse 4?
2. Although we go through periods of testing and trials, by faith we live. No problems we encounter in this life change what has been established in heaven. What is the ultimate result of our faith?

Simple Prayer: When nothing seems familiar, turn my face toward You, Lord.

Day 54
A Sweet Resolution

Your Heart's Cry

I need a quick release. At least one hour of relief from everything. What started as a glass of wine with dinner has escalated to a bottle of wine every night. Sometimes that isn't even enough to dull the sensation of emptiness. Sometimes even it fails to fill up the vacancy I feel inside. You don't have to tell me I have a problem, I know I have a problem. Your accusations only drive me deeper into my cave of isolation. Don't tell me to just stop. If I could, I would. This hunger is bigger than I am. I hate what this does to me, but I can't stop inflicting this pain.

Dear friends, I urge you, as foreigners and exiles, to abstain from sinful desires, which wage war against your soul. **1 Peter 2:11 NIV**

His Reply

Ask for My help. There are some battles you will never win alone. This is one such battle. This battle will require you to lean heavily upon Me to deliver you from misplaced cravings. What you are drawn to is only a substitute for what you truly desire. Peace cannot be found in a bottle, a needle, a drug, or food. The peace you seek can only be found in Me. Willpower can only do so much. Ask Me to step in where your willpower ends. I am the sweet resolution you are longing for.

Be baptized into the liberty and peace of My presence. Just as when the Israelites crossed over the Red Sea, and their enemies were consumed by the rushing waters, so shall it be with your addictive enemies of the past. Let my uncompromising love and acceptance envelop you and watch your enemies drown in My presence. I have given you an abundance of peace to walk in. You will walk with a shield of My glory. My glory shall remind you daily that you have been chosen and redeemed.

Therefore, if anyone is in Christ, he is a new creation. The old has passed away; behold, the new has come. **2 Corinthians 5:17 ESV**

Scripture: Matthew 6:7-13

Going Deeper Questions:

1. Prayer is simply a conversation with God, but at times we make it more complicated than it really is. Thankfully, Jesus gave us some guidelines to use when we pray. What major areas of our life does The Lord's Prayer address?

2. Isn't it comforting to know the Father knows what we need, even before we ask? Why then do you think He requires us to ask for His help? What does asking reveal about our relationship with God?

Simple Prayer: God, deliver me from temptation.

Day 55
The Changing Beat

*Y*our **Heart's Cry**

I don't feel well. Illness and disease have become my daily task. Pill bottles line my nightstand and fill my morning cup. My day is marked by the pain of this journey. Sickness has become the badge I wear, my defining feature. Don't ask me how I'm doing if you don't want to hear the truth. I'm not fine. I'm broken and burdened by my afflictions. My ailments may be invisible to you, but they are the centerpiece of all I say, feel, and do.

The name of the LORD is a strong tower; The righteous runs into it and is safe. **Proverbs 18:10 NASB**

*H*is **Reply**

Do not be afraid when sickness comes to your body, and do not yield your peace to the symptoms that plague you. Take time to rest and to be restored both physically and spiritually. You have endured a great deal of stress in your circumstances and environment, and these stressful situations have taken their toll. Allow Me to bring healing and restoration. Be deliberate in releasing anxiety and seeking My face. I am able to bring healing where there was sickness and disease. Be bold and very courageous as you turn to Me when fear tries to overtake you. I have been touched with the feeling of your infirmities, and through that suffering, I now have the power to deliver you from every dilemma and heal your every wound and disease. Remember, I am responsible for you in every way. Trust Me to protect, provide, nurture, guide, heal, and deliver you.

Beloved, I pray that in all respects you may prosper and be in good health, just as your soul prospers. **3 John 1:2 NASB**

Scripture: Matthew 4:23-24

Going Deeper Questions:

1. A large portion of the ministry of Jesus was that of The Great Physician. He spent many hours doing "house calls." Why do you feel healing was such an important part of Jesus' ministry?

2. How is healing part of the Good News He brought to the crowds? What are the different types of healing He offers? What healing are you in need of today?

Simple Prayer: Lord, heal my mind, body, and spirit.

Day 56
Empty Arms

*Y*our Heart's Cry

Another announcement, another baby shower, another visit to the baby aisle to look, long, and languish. Everyone seems to be getting pregnant but me. Every month, I battle with my hopes. Pulling every desire to the surface as we try once again. Rejoicing every time I'm late in expectation of the baby to come, only to be let down days later. In the back of my mind, I wonder if there is something wrong with me. Why am I not fruitful? Why is this blessing being denied? My arms ache for the warmth of a tiny frame to hold. My heart burns from the love penned up inside, awaiting the new life I pray will one day come.

And by faith even Sarah, who was past childbearing age, was enabled to bear children because she considered him faithful who had made the promise. **Hebrews 11:11 NIV**

*H*is Reply

The longing in your heart is one to nurture and to love. Birth comes in many forms. This season of waiting has already birthed much within you. Out of this time has come a deeper dependence on Me. From this season has come a greater level of spiritual maturity and conviction. Do not resent those who you see walking in the blessing you desire. Rejoice with those who are rejoicing. When you can't understand My plan, trust My heart. Blessings are not being denied you, but some blessings may not arrive as you would expect. Allow My plan to guide your steps toward filling this empty place.

He gives the barren woman a home, making her the joyous mother of children. Praise the LORD! **Psalm 113:9 ESV**

Scripture: Philippians 4:11-15

Going Deeper Questions:

1. Contentment allows you to be at peace in a situation. One of the hardest parts of infertility is finding a way to be content while waiting. How can the period of waiting be used by God to draw you closer to Him?

2. Our strength is from the Lord. The closer we become to Him, the stronger we become. How does our relationship with Christ enable us to do "all things"?

Simple Prayer: I surrender my desire to have a child to You, Lord.

Day 57
A Deep Ache

Your Heart's Cry

A discord arises in my spirit and questions float into my mind on a sea of torment. What if I end it all now? My depression has set me on a roller-coaster ride of emotions with no brakes. I don't see any other way. I'm numb to Your words and prayers. Guilt and shame eat away at my soul, bind my views of life, and kill everything inside of me that dares risk to hope. I hate who I am. The alarms in my head ring loud to proclaim loser, failure, not enough. All I want is for this pain to stop. I'm not courting death. I only want to end the pain of this life. Deep sleep is the only solution for this deep ache.

For the enemy has pursued my soul; he has crushed my life to the ground; he has made me sit in darkness like those long dead. Therefore my spirit faints within me; my heart within me is appalled. **Psalm 143:3-4 ESV**

His Reply

Do not give up, and do not give into the lie that there is no other way to relieve the pain. Your pain is real, and I acknowledge it. But, will you acknowledge Me as the One who can heal your deepest ache? Every life will have ups and downs; no one is immune. This valley is only a stop in the journey of your life. Do not set up camp here. Keep walking through it, and you will find your way out. The way out of this depression is to keep moving. Keep walking in My direction. Keep moving towards those I send to give you counsel and guidance. Every day is one day closer to coming out on the other side of this. You are winning this mental battle, and you will win if you stay the course.

You have already won in ways that cannot be seen just now. I know you are tempted to stop hoping, but do not. Events ahead will give a glimpse of the blessings to come. They will be enough to encourage you, but not enough to show the full picture. You will still have to lean heavily on Me. You will still have to stay close by My side. This season will build mountain-moving faith if you keep moving forward. You do have a choice. Choose to trust Me to guide you to the healing only I can provide.

This illness does not lead to death. It is for the glory of God, so that the Son of God may be glorified through it. **John 11:4 ESV**

Scripture: 2 Corinthians 1:8–10

*G*oing **Deeper Questions:**
1. Even Paul had times in his life when he felt he had received a death sentence. In verses 9 and 10, what revelation did he have about his feelings?
2. Christ alone is able to lift us out of our despair. If you have ever had thoughts of suicide, what pulled you back from the edge of death? If you currently have thoughts of suicide, talk with someone you trust about your feelings. Also, share your heart's cry with God. Share your pain with Him, then take a moment to listen to what He whispers to your heart.
Simple Prayer: Show me a better way to ease the pain, Lord.

Day 58
Pressured

*Y*our **Heart's Cry**

Not one more thing. Not one more homework page to be checked. Not one more load of laundry to be done. Not another bill that needs to be paid. Not another person requiring anything from me. Not one more batch of cupcakes for the bake sale. Not one more hour of my time at work. Not one more appointment added to my calendar. Nothing, nada, zilch. If one more thing tries to squeeze into the tight space of my strained emotions and maxed out schedule, I will implode.

I saw the Lord always before me. Because he is at my right hand, I will not be shaken. **Acts 2:25 NIV**

*H*is **Reply**

Beloved, you have forgotten I came to change your life. I came so you could live an abundant life, overflowing, and to the fullest. The full life I desire for you is not one of more daily pressures, but one of abiding grace to accomplish all I ask of you. Some of your activities are your plan and not a part of My plan. Ask Me to help you discern the difference. Be free from the bondage of external pressures and expectations. Some of these expectations are even self-imposed because of your desire to gain approval and acceptance from others. Now is the time when you can be free from the stress of trying to please others, not through an attitude of rebellion, but rather an attitude of submission to truth. Enter into the rest of following My heart as I lead you beyond the limits of soul and flesh. Staying too busy has led you into a pit of stress and bitterness. I have the power to rescue you from every pit you have fallen into.

Trouble and distress have come upon me, but your commands give me delight. **Psalm 119:143 NIV**

Scripture: Haggai 1:5-11

Going Deeper Questions:

1. When life becomes so hectic, it leaves little time for reflection, which is exactly when time for reflection is most needed. Twice in this small passage of scripture, God admonishes us to give careful thought to our ways. Why is taking the time to consider the "why" of our activities an important part of stress management?

2. Stress is our reminder to go back to the basics, re-evaluate our priorities, and bring them in line with God's plan for our life. What are your current priorities? Do they bring you a sense of fulfillment and joy? If not, seek God for guidance on what changes need to be made.

Simple Prayer: Relieve the stress and pressure surrounding my days, Lord.

Day 59
Dwindling Strength

*Y*our Heart's Cry

I dread stepping out of this bed. Lying here affords me a level of comfort I rarely experience once I arise. I'm tired. Not simply "I need a nap" tired, but "I need a break from my life" tired. My energy is drained. My strength has expired. The effort required to hope is too much to ask. Doctors find nothing wrong with me, but something is definitely wrong. I can't run another step of this rat's race. I'm chronically fatigued, emotionally listless, and spiritually indifferent. So I lay here staring at the ceiling. I stay immobile, fixated in my weakness, and anchored to disgrace.

He gives strength to the weary and increases the power of the weary. **Isaiah 40:29 NIV**

*H*is Reply

Be strong. The strength you desire is already in you. Claim what is already yours. You are amazing. I knew one day you would fall, and I would have to catch you. Allow Me to stretch forth My wings and teach you more lessons on how to fly high and go far on the warm winds of My Spirit. Take time to quiet your mind and emotions in the midst of turmoil and demands, and I will give you peace in the midst of your own private storm. Be strong in the assurance of My strength and presence. This is an exercise in trusting and resting, no extra effort required. Allow My strength to be made perfect in your weakness. Once you fully realize I am here for you, you are free to fully explore the freedom of your choices and assignments from Me.

The LORD is my strength and my shield; in him my heart trusts, and I am helped; my heart exults, and with my song I give thanks to him. **Psalm 28:7 ESV**

Scripture: Psalm 16:1-5

Going Deeper Questions:

1. Running after things that do not satisfy can be exhausting. Anything that becomes more important than God becomes a god in our life. What other gods have you chased after?

2. There is only one true and living God. Did these other gods satisfy you or leave you disappointed? How is the Lord alone your portion and inheritance?

Simple Prayer: Energize me with Your strength, Lord.

Day 60
In the Spin Cycle

Your Heart's Cry

If I could stop, I would. But the frantic spinning that is my life is outpacing my ability to keep up. I'm caught in a maze of confusion and worry, circling the same spot and expecting to see something I have not seen. Pacing down the same road and expecting to find a different outcome. My compulsion compels me to check again, clean better, hoard more, and hide it all well enough that you think I fit in. This propensity to perfect has set me on a course with no real destination.

What you have learned and received and heard and seen in me—practice these things, and the God of peace will be with you.
Philippians 4:9 ESV

His Reply

The release of grace, mercy, and peace in your days can change everything. I hold all the keys to every door, lock, and obstacle imaginable. It's easy to get caught up in the commotion of events surrounding you and forget I am the answer to every problem. I am the peace in every storm. There is not one issue too big or too small for Me to overcome. Rely on Me when you are down and out. Look to Me when you are fearful and distressed. Turn to Me before you have reached the point of finding that everything else has already or will eventually fail. I am the way out.

Grace, mercy, and peace will be with us, from God the Father and from Jesus Christ the Father's Son, in truth and love. **2 John 1:3 ESV**

Scripture: Ephesians 3:17-21

Going Deeper Questions:
1. Jesus wants to make His home in our hearts so He can reveal to you the magnitude of God's love. It is this love that completes us. What obsessions and worries threaten to overtake your heart today? Allow His love to reclaim every area of your heart.
2. God is able to do so much more than we can ask or even think. Nothing surprises Him. What comfort does this bring your weary mind?

Simple Prayer: God, ease my worries and remove the stronghold of my obsessions.

Positive Emotions

Day 61
Hope Happens

Your Heart's Cry

I remember when I lost all hope. Slipping into a deep, endless pool of pity. Hitting the bottom of my supply. Grabbing at the first lifeline I could find. It was in this place that hope happened. Waiting in the silence, hope appeared. It was here You extended a hand toward me. It was here I found out who You really are. When life got hard, You were my soft landing. When trouble surrounded me, You were my way out. So I will quietly wait when things do not go my way, and I will look for Your extended hand.

But as for me, I will always have hope; I will praise you more and more. **Psalm 71:14 NIV**

His Reply

The difficulties you faced in the past slowly chipped away at the foundation of your hope and faith. But, this is a time of restoration. Hope makes all things possible. It is a deposit bearing witness of My goodness to come. Hope is a song with a rich melody. It causes your spirit to rejoice, even before you catch the tune. It bears witness to the things on the horizon. It testifies of the unlimited potential of this life. Hope is a certainty, a promise that endures. Hope is a steadfast assurance of dreams that can still appear. Hope is looking at Me face-to-face and beckoning Me to draw near. My hope will never leave you helpless or alone. My hope is the answer to every test, every trial, and every difficulty.

Return to your fortress, you prisoners of hope; even now I announce that I will restore twice as much to you. **Zechariah 9:12 NIV**

Scripture: Lamentations 3:19-33

*G*oing **Deeper Questions:**

1. When you think back on the lowest points in your life, what happened on the inside of you when hope first appeared? How does hope change your outlook?

2. Running from pain only creates a different kind of pain. Why is it necessary to confront pain and trouble directly? What treasures can be found when you allow your pain to breathe?

Simple Prayer: Maintain my hope at all times, for You are my Living Hope, Lord.

Day 62
Peace Like a River

Your **Heart's Cry**

I am pressed on all sides. Stress pushes back against my happiness, shoving it away. The struggle continues day in and day out. Shaken by the onslaught of commotion, my mind fights to find something to cling to. Rocking against the hard backboard of a life framed in tribulation. Still I stand, frozen in anticipation of the help to come. Swaddled in Your covenant and cloaked in Your grace. I step out in eager expectation, grasping Your hand as I take my place. I know this ride may be dangerous, but with You my resolve is resolute. I am looking beyond my circumstances and looking right into the deep places of Your heart.

I have said these things to you, that in me you may have peace. In the world you will have tribulation. But take heart; I have overcome the world. **John 16:33 ESV**

His **Reply**

Be at rest in every circumstance. I am not your situation. I am Lord of Lords and King of Kings. I created all that is and all that will ever be. I am not moved by your situation. I am moved by your faith. When events come to steal your peace, choose to press into My presence. In Me, you will find safety and rest. Focus your attention on Me instead of your problems. Peace is not just the absence of trouble; it is a quiet and calm heart. Peace carries an ease of flow and existence. Peace is not rushed, nor is it laborious. Peace pauses and inhales in the moment. Peace sits in the tranquil waters and echoes the voice of silence. Peace breaks the bondage of busyness and releases a reverential hush. My peace is yours.

Peace I leave with you, my peace I give unto you: not as the world giveth, give I unto you. Let not your heart be troubled, neither let it be afraid. **John 14:27 KJV**

Scripture: Philippians 4:4-7

*G*oing **Deeper Questions:**

1. Philippians 4:4 begins by encouraging you to celebrate God day and night. How can celebrating God lead to greater peace in your life?

2. God wants to know what we are feeling. When we shape our worries into prayers, we begin to speak in a language that moves His heart. What promises can be found in this passage of scripture for those who choose prayer over worry?

Simple Prayer: Place Your peace in my heart, God.

Day 63
Awakening Joy

Your Heart's Cry

I've chased after happiness and pursued it as my own, but the chase has been hard, and I am undone. Forced smiles shape my lips. Pain is pushed aside. I try to choose to be uplifting, but it's a false happiness I've found. The happiness I've been taught is one of positive affirmations and declarations. The happiness I've learned is based on the feelings I can force into submission. This is not the joy I seek. I seek the joy You promise, the one present at all time. But how can joy come in the morning if I've cried throughout the night? Present to me the gift of this joy, and I will open it with delight.

You make known to me the path of life; you will fill me with joy in your presence, with eternal pleasures at your right hand. **Psalm 16:11 NIV**

His Reply

Happiness is only a shadow of the joy you seek. It is a shallow imposter of what you really need. The joy I give is not an emotion limited to your success, desires, and well-being. My joy is independent of your emotions. My joy comes upon the dawning of revelation and light. It does not rely upon your temperament or mood. Happiness may be a choice, but joy simply is. It cannot be manufactured or faked. You do not have to dig deep to find it; you just have to walk in. Joy is one of My gifts to you. It is the byproduct of a life restored. It is yours with no strings attached because it is a settled issue. It is magnified by the truth and reality of the work that has already been done in your life. Joy is the real objective evidence of restoration and being restored to who you were designed to be.

I have no greater joy than to hear that my children are walking in the truth. **3 John 1:4 ESV**

Scripture: Psalm 92:1-5

Going Deeper Questions:
1. Happiness is not joy. How does remembering who God is and what He has done position our hearts to be joyful?
2. Restoration occurs when something is returned to its proper condition. How then is being restored to the Lord necessary to have true joy?

Simple Prayer: Make my joy complete, Lord.

Day 64
Passionate Awe

*Y*our Heart's Cry

You alone are God. The heavens declare Your glory. The seas testify of Your power. Each living being was created by You alone. I marvel at the beauty of all You have made. I am in awe of who you are, and I've just begun to scratch the surface. My heart is full. Who can truly know You in all your power? No one can compare. I stand amazed by You. When I am unsure of tomorrow, remind me You are Almighty, and in You sit all my tomorrows.

All this also comes from the LORD Almighty, wonderful in counsel and magnificent in wisdom. **Isaiah 28:29 NIV**

*H*is Reply

Nothing within My creation can fully reveal the measure of My love. It is for this reason I came. I, the Creator, stepped into all I created as an act of love. This is what love is. Love is patient. Love is kind. Love holds no account of right or wrong. Love endures all. Love led Me to the cross. Love took Me into the grave, and love refused to allow Me to stay in the tomb. When nothing else could suffice, love overcame.

I love you with an everlasting love, a love that cannot fail and will not fade. You are precious in My sight, for you are My temple, My place of habitation. I am calling you into greater closeness and more intimacy than you have known before. I do not want you to become lukewarm about our relationship. May your time in My presence stir the cooling embers and cause the coals to become a roaring flame. May the resurrecting power of My love be a living reality in your life.

For we are God's handiwork, created in Christ Jesus to do good works, which God prepared in advance for us to do. **Ephesians 2:10 NIV**

Scripture: John 15:10-17

*G*oing **Deeper Questions:**

1. The Savior of the world hung on a cross for you, an act often referred to as "the passion." How was the cross an act of passion?

2. You are chosen by God, pursued by His love, and destined to be in relationship with Him. What do these actions say about the type of love God has towards you? How does that make you feel?

Simple Prayer: Stir the embers of my heart to burn more of You, Lord.

Day 65
Balanced Serenity

*Y*our Heart's Cry

Noise has become my daily companion. The sounds of life invade my quiet space, beating on the door of my serenity. Silence is a rare commodity. In the stillness of the night, after all have gone to bed, I steal away a few moments to myself. I breathe deeply in the stillness of the moment. I exhale the tension of the day. All the balls I've juggled fall softly around me; not one of them crashes to the ground. You are my soft landing. Your grace, the buoyancy in my sinking emotions. A calm visits me in these moments as I balance the weight of this life against Your faithfulness.

Then the LORD said to me, "You have seen well, for I am watching over my word to perform it." **Jeremiah 1:12 ESV**

*H*is Reply

Find your place in Me. When life and family pull you in numerous directions, find your grace place. Let Me establish your schedule. I know what is coming, and I know the importance of your activities better than you. Make a move towards silent reflection during times of stress. Lay your burdens by the banks and walk into the calm river of My steadfastness. Trust Me to be able to uphold you. Walk out ankle deep and test the waters. As your cares are met with understanding, wade out further until you are knee-deep in My favor. Then, recline back and allow My presence to carry you. You can never drown in the ocean of My grace towards you.

When you pass through the waters, I will be with you; and through the rivers, they shall not overwhelm you; when you walk through fire you shall not be burned, and the flame shall not consume you. **Isaiah 43:2 ESV**

Scripture: Isaiah 48:17-18

*G*oing **Deeper Questions:**

1. Life has been called one big classroom. Everything has the potential to be part of the lesson plan. In what way is the Bible our textbook for life?

2. Swimming is difficult if you fear the water. How is resting in God's peace similar to floating on water?

Simple Prayer: Uphold me with Your faithfulness, O God.

Day 66
Empowering Contentment

Your Heart's Cry

In my need, I see the glass as half empty. Yet, my heart knows You can fill it. In my fear, I see the threat as imminent. Yet, my mind knows this is a false reality. In my doubt, I see the chances of change as impossible. Yet, my spirit testifies with You that all things are possible. So I will stand defiantly and declare, "It is well with my soul." I speak to every fear, "I will not be afraid." I proclaim to every doubt, "My Lord has healed my unbelief." I shout to every need, "I shall not want." I am empowered, equipped, and encouraged by You, through You, and in You.

For where your treasure is, there your heart will be also.
Matthew 6:21 ESV

His Reply

Do not fear uncertain times, for I am with you. I have chosen you as My own, and I will establish you. I will take hold of your hand and be your constant companion. Strength will arise inside of you as you shift to a new level of trust in Me. Through My strength, you will receive the power to shift from constantly striving into abiding rest. In contentment, you will find rest from your labor. I know of every need you have. I am not moved by need; I am moved by faith. This is not about you working more to achieve more. It's about you leaving room for the miraculous in your life.

For the gifts and the calling of God are irrevocable.
Romans 11:29 ESV

Scripture: 1Timothy 6:6-8

Going Deeper Questions:

1. Contentment is a gift with great gain. How does being content help guard our heart against envy, jealousy, and discouragement?
2. Food and clothing are the most basic elements needed for survival. Why do you think the Bible focused on these two in this scripture?

Simple Prayer: Lord, show me how to live with trusting contentment.

Day 67
Optimistic Faith

*Y*our Heart's Cry

What has faith without works cost me? Knowledge of Your blessings builds up the ruins of this broken temple. Life is breathed in my spirit, and I believe things can be better. But, the fear of a setback holds me back. So I do nothing. Instead of positive progression toward Your desired outcome, I fall back into what is familiar and common. What was once my comfort zone has become too small for the God-size dream You have placed inside me.

And He said to them, "Because of the littleness of your faith; for truly I say to you, if you have faith as a mustard seed, you shall say to this mountain, 'Move from here to there,' and it shall move; and nothing shall be impossible to you." **Matthew 17:20 NASB**

*H*is Reply

Faith without works is dead. Faith will always be tested. The test is not to trick you in going back or into giving up, but to promote you into another level of maturity. Maturity is evidenced by your response and your attitude during the test. Remember, you surrendered to believing in Me and to living a different life. This life is about taking up your cross. This life is about faith and blessings. This life is about taking what little faith you have and holding onto it until you see the manifestation of the blessing.

Worry and doubt kill faith. Rise up with faith that reaches

out and calls those things that are not as though they were. Cast aside your unbelief and your doubt, and expect optimistically. Watch for opportunities to launch out in faith and do what I've given you to do. Be courageous, and refuse to allow fear to keep you from My highest and best. You will be changed from glory to glory, from encounter to encounter, and from faith to faith.

But my righteous one will live by faith. **Hebrews 10:38 NIV**

Scripture: Mark 8:34-37

*G*oing Deeper Questions:

1. It takes optimistic faith to deny yourself and take up your cross. How is losing your life in Christ the only way to save it?
2. Striving to be more and have more can cost more than you're willing to pay. What is your answer to the question, "What does it profit a man to gain the whole world and forfeit his soul?"

Simple Prayer: Move mountains with my mustard-seed faith, Lord.

Day 68
Wild Patience

Your Heart's Cry

I sit in the waiting room of my life. Convinced of the appointment, but I've not been called to the forefront. Time passes. I flip through the old as I await the new. Expired words feed my mind. I need fresh revelation for the new place I need to go. So, while I wait, I'll stay encouraged in You, Lord. I will use my gifts now in the waiting room and hone my talents. I will not waste what You have placed inside me. Your callings are irrevocable, so I know this waiting room is just for an allotted time.

But those who wait on the Lord shall renew their strength; They shall mount up with wings like eagles. They shall run and not be weary, They shall walk and not faint. **Isaiah 40:31 NKJV**

His Reply

Patience is faith that prevails, overcomes, and has victory in the midst of inactivity. Patiently wait with the expectation to receive the promise. Look through My eyes. It isn't about what you see. It's about what I see. What you see is not bad, but it does not have the full scope of understanding. This is why you wait on Me. My ways are higher than your ways. Wait until you see from My point of view. Wait until you feel a shift on the inside, a shift towards faith. The spiritual change on the inside is the precursor to the things you desire to see on the outside.

Learn by way of patience to sit before Me. Let patience have its perfect work, that you may be complete and lacking nothing.

As the heavens are higher than the earth, so are my ways higher than your ways and my thoughts than your thoughts. **Isaiah 55:9 NIV**

Scripture: Psalm 37:4-7

*G*oing **Deeper Questions:**

1. Finding joy in the Lord is a way to constantly stay in a positive attitude. What can you do to delight yourself in the Lord?

2. Being still before the Lord can be challenging in an age of constant activity and endless avenues for communication. How can patience be a wild act?

Simple Prayer: I choose to wait on Your timing, Lord.

Day 69
Loving Kindness

Your Heart's Cry

Every good student wants to pass the test. I want to see the Father's face. I want to make Him proud. But, some tests were harder than I imagined. There was no study guide. I had no time to prepare. There were surprises thrown in that caught me off guard and threw me off track. All I can whisper as I turn the page on this hard assignment is, "Teacher, did I pass the test?" I know I didn't get an 'A', but did I do well enough to move to the next level? Did I respond as one who has spent time in Your presence? Did my actions show love and kindness? Were my words Your words? Did my answers speak of life and not death? Am I ready to advance?

For His lovingkindness is great toward us, And the truth of the LORD is everlasting. Praise the LORD! **Psalm 117:2 NASB**

His Reply

Quiet your soul, for this testing is only for a moment. Now is not the time to give up; it is a time to establish yourself in faith and obedience to My leading. The lessons of this season are of great value and will produce good fruit, but you must rise above the point of your own victimization and yield to My work in you. When temptations arise to draw you into conflict, do not take the bait. Guard your heart and your mouth and be willing to walk away without expressing your dissatisfaction or disagreement. Come to Me during the test. Allow Me to remind you of what you know to be right and true. You are prepared to overcome and come forth in victory. Every test will work to your advantage and strengthen your position if you will yield to the work of My Spirit in the testing.

Do not let kindness and truth leave you; Bind them around your neck, Write them on the tablet of your heart. **Proverbs 3:3 NASB**

Scripture: Psalm 103:2-5

*G*oing **Deeper Questions:**

1. You've heard the saying, "membership has its privileges." Likewise, following Jesus has its benefits. What are some of the benefits mentioned in verse 2?

2. Our part of receiving those benefits lies in being able to bless the Lord at all times and realizing our circumstances do not change who He is. When in your life has it been difficult to bless the Lord? Pick one scripture to put in your spiritual safe deposit box to withdraw in times of difficulty. Write it out, post it in a prominent place, and meditate on it for the next seven days.

Simple Prayer: May I learn the lesson in every test the first time I go through it, Lord.

Day 70
In Pursuit of Delight

Your Heart's Cry

I'm captivated by joy and moved by the need to appease the emptiness I feel inside. Every empty place, every heartache has me on an endless chase. Pursuing something I cannot articulate, yet fully aware of its absence and scarred by its delay. I've searched my whole life, looking for what can only be found in the Son. Only You can satisfy the longing and fulfill the desires of my heart. You are the open door to all I seek. You are the song my heart wants to sing. I'm looking to You to be my guide. As I follow hard after You and stretch to grasp Your garment's hem, turn Your gaze upon me and speak the words I need to hear.

My sheep listen to my voice; I know them, and they follow me.
John 10:27 NIV

His Reply

Continue to pursue and you will find that the One you are pursuing has been pursuing you all this time. With patience, I have waited for you to hear Me in your pain—speaking words of comfort and decreeing you will soon experience better days. With joy, I have anticipated the revelations you will uncover and with My goodness, I have lifted the limitations off your future. The disappointments of the past are not a reflection of what I have for you. Stretch your expectation and believe the best is yet to come. Run fully towards Me and press against the crowd.

Your pursuit will always be rewarded by My glory coming down.

One thing I ask of the LORD, this is what I seek: that I may dwell in the house of the LORD all the days of my life, to gaze upon the beauty of the LORD and to seek him in his temple. **Psalm 27:4 NIV**

Scripture: Psalm 139:1-10

*G*oing **Deeper Questions:**

1. You are known by God. Long before you thought about Him, He was already thinking about you. What times in your life did you feel you had gone too far for God to be able to find you? Can you see His presence in those times now?

2. The right hand of God is the hand where Jesus sits making intercession for us. This is the same hand with which He leads and holds us. What can you hear Jesus interceding with the Father on your behalf about today?

Simple Prayer: Thank You for passionately pursuing me, Lord.

Gratitude

Day 71
After the Rain

*Y*our Heart's Cry

I wait in anticipation for the rain to come. Although I have not seen an outpouring, I believe it is possible. I believe You are able to do exceedingly and abundantly above all I can ask or think. I believe tomorrow does not have to be like yesterday. I believe a sudden, unprecedented blessing is possible. Just because it has not happened yet in my life does not mean it cannot happen. I know You are able. So, I will wait on You, Lord, for I know You are the Supplier of all of my needs.

Who covers the heavens with clouds, Who provides rain for the earth, Who makes grass to grow on the mountains. **Psalm 147:8 NASB**

*H*is Reply

I have storehouses you do not know about. My supply is unlimited. Every promise has a proper time. Trust Me to open the floodgates and rain down My mercies and My blessings upon your life in due season. Continue yielding to Me a heart of anticipation and expectation. Stay in a mindset of gratitude. Your faithfulness to believe even when you have not seen is in itself an act of worship. Stay faithful, trusting, and hopeful. Make every effort to be ready when the rain comes, because it will surely come.

The LORD will open the heavens, the storehouse of his bounty, to send rain on your land in season and to bless all the work of your hands. **Deuteronomy 28:12 NIV**

Scripture: 1 Kings 18:41-46

Going Deeper Questions:

1. Waiting can lead to depression and hopelessness. When were times in your life waiting became the source of your pain and discomfort?

2. Have you experienced a season of drought in your life? How did hearing the sound of rain position you to be ready to receive? How did you feel after the rain came?

Simple Prayer: Help me hear the sound of abundant rain as I wait on You, Lord.

Day 72
Surprised by Freedom

*Y*our Heart's Cry

The chains of the past have been broken. I feel the stirring of liberty surrounding me. I can move again. Free to dance like no one's watching. Free to sing like no one's listening. But, I know You are there. You are there in the quiet moments, twirling me in my dance of liberty. You are there in the times of jubilant joy, relishing the rhythm of my song. You have always been there. Watching me. Listening to me. You have always been there waiting for opportunities to surprise me, and now You have surprised me with the gift of freedom.

For freedom Christ has set us free; stand firm therefore, and do not submit again to a yoke of slavery. **Galatians 5:1 ESV**

*H*is Reply

You were created to live in liberty. You were designed for freedom. As the wind blows uninhibited, and no one knows which way it will go, so is My Spirit. My Spirit also resides in you to breathe freedom into your heart. You were once a prisoner to sin, bound by your shame and guilt. But those who have been set free are truly free. They are free from the bondage of sin and free to live a full and overflowing life. Now that you are free, make sure you stay free. Do not be tied up again by the shackles of sin. Dance fearlessly into My presence and know you are welcome to come in and out as you please. You are free in Me.

Now the Lord is the Spirit, and where the Spirit of the Lord is, there is freedom. **2 Corinthians 3:17 ESV**

Scripture: Romans 6:1-14

Going Deeper Questions:

1. Freedom in Christ does not mean we are free to sin, but that we are free from the bondage of sin. How is death to the sin in your life the beginning of a new life in Christ?
2. By grace, we are set free. What are some areas of your life you now feel the stirring of liberty?

Simple Prayer: May freedom be my portion in You, Lord.

Day 73
A Rainbow of My Own

*Y*our Heart's Cry

I am standing on Your promises. Building my dreams in a world of doubt, yet I believe You are faithful. Even when I have not seen what You have said, I know Your word is truth, and Your promises are mine. Help me during my times of unbelief. Help me release my striving and find your peace. I surrender my need to be in control. I have found You are my all in all. As I search the sky for evidence of a shift, fulfill each promise as you wish. Imaginative and creative God, paint my horizons with a rainbow of my own. Ribbons of colorful hues and shades, beautiful reminders of Your amazing grace.

By which he has granted to us his precious and very great promises, so that through them you may become partakers of the divine nature, having escaped from the corruption that is in the world because of sinful desire. **2 Peter 1:4 ESV**

*H*is Reply

In a world of uncertainty, pain, and struggle, I am your unshakable truth and blessed assurance. I am your covering, and I have given you a canopy of promises. My promises are your shelter from the rain clouds of this life. They protect you from a downpour of hopelessness and unbelief. Cling to each promise you find in My Word. Each has a specific goal and can heal a specific hurt. Make My promises your dwelling place. My

promises are true, and they are for you. Look for them to come in the wake of your storm clouds. When you see a rainbow in the sky, know that I have penetrated through the darkness to bring you beauty and light.

And now I am about to go the way of all the earth, and you know in your hearts and souls, all of you, that not one word has failed of all the good things that the Lord your God promised concerning you. All have come to pass for you; not one of them has failed. **Joshua 23:14 ESV**

Scripture: Psalm 18:30-33

Going Deeper Questions:
1. Rainbows are beautiful arcs in the sky that remind us of God's promises. How can umbrellas also be a reminder of the promises of God?
2. Having your feet secure on a "high place" gives you an up close and personal view of your rainbow. What promises are you clinging to today?

Simple Prayer: Remind me of Your promises, Lord.

Day 74
Seasons of the Heart

*Y*our Heart's Cry

The cold surrounded me, but You did not allow it to freeze my heart. With the warmth of Your love, You held me. You held me through the darkest hours. You held me when I didn't want to be held. You took me by the hand and lovingly guided me through the congested streets of my fears. You would not allow me to go back. Daily, You pointed me toward Your promises. With Your eyes, You directed me. Therefore, I will stay close to You. I will stay in a position near Your heart, listening to its beat. I will stay in a position of yielded trust, dependent upon this one truth: You are good. So even when the pain is great, even when I don't know if I can take my next breath, even when I see no good in the situation, I will trust You. Your goodness does not change; it remains.

I the LORD do not change. **Malachi 3:6 NIV**

*H*is Reply

It is My desire to let My goodness surround you. It is My plan for you to be a carrier of My glory. Take My presence into every place you go. Bring warmth into the cold, dark places of life. Take light into the dimly lit places of pain. Take peace into the tumultuous storms of a fallen world. Take hope into the raging attacks against your joy. Make My presence your resting place. Settle once and for all in your mind who I am. I am good, and My mercy and loving-kindness endure forever. I am your reward. I am your crowning treasure. I AM WHO I AM.

Give thanks to the Lord, for he is good, for his steadfast love endures forever. **Psalm 136:1 ESV**

Scripture: Psalm 32:1-11

Going Deeper Questions:
1. In The Message Bible, Psalm 32:1 says, "Count yourself lucky, how happy you must be—you get a fresh start, your slate's wiped clean." No matter what has transpired in our life, God gives us second chances. What does having your slate wiped clean mean to you? How is this necessary to have a fresh start? In what ways can past hurt emotions stand in the way of that second chance?

2. Holding nothing back from God opens up a pathway for genuine communication, relationship, and intimacy. It is the only way this core relationship can be fully healed and restored. Now that you have gotten years of hurt emotions off your chest, what physical changes have you noted in your body? Celebrate the work God is doing in your life today.

Simple Prayer: Lord, You are good, and I praise Your Holy Name.

Day 75
The Life of the Redeemed

*Y*our Heart's Cry

I will tell all who will listen about the change in my life. I am fearfully and wonderfully made. I am no longer a captive to the past. I am a new creature. The old attitudes, habits, mindsets, and fears have passed away, and I see life through the lens of faith. I believe You love me, and You came to the Earth as a baby. I believe You went to the cross and died for me. You suffered so I did not have to. You gave Your life, so I can have eternal life. So, I thank You and praise You, Lord, for the great love You have for me. It is with joy I go forth and declare, "I've been redeemed."

My lips will shout for joy, when I sing praises to you; my soul also, which you have redeemed. **Psalm 71:23 ESV**

*H*is Reply

Your heart of praise releases a beautiful fragrance to Me. But believe Me when I say you were worth everything. You were worth the humiliation of being paraded through the streets. You were worth the taunting, the beatings, and the harassment. You were worth the lashes I took upon My back. You were worth each nail hammered into My hands and feet. You were worth every drop of blood I shed on Calvary. You were worth it even before you came to Me. I loved you long before you cleaned up your act. I loved you when your life was a mess. See, it is not

what you do that makes Me love you. I love you for who you are, all of you. I love the part that still messes up sometimes, and I love the part of you that desires to live rightly. My love is unconditional, unearned, and cannot be deserved. I give it to you freely, no matter what your current state. So, live your life knowing you do not have to be perfect and always right. I am your Redeemer, forever by your side.

In all their affliction He was afflicted, And the angel of His presence saved them; In His love and in His mercy He redeemed them, And He lifted them and carried them all the days of old. **Isaiah 63:9 NASB**

Scripture: Psalm 107:1-8

*G*oing **Deeper Questions:**

1. Psalm 107 begins by imploring those of us who have been redeemed by the Lord to speak out and tell others about what the Lord has done. Why is it important that the redeemed say so?

2. Praise is when we proclaim the goodness of God. Why should praise be a common practice in the life of the redeemed?

Simple Prayer: God, daily remind me that my Redeemer lives.

Day 76
The Well-Tended Garden

*Y*our Heart's Cry

I'm depending on You, Lord. Discern my needs and touch my life as only You can. Fill the dry places that thirst for a deep watering of Your truths. Pull up the weeds that prevent me from fully partaking in Your goodness. Then, walk through Your garden and rearrange things as You see fit. Sample the fruit You find and see if it is good. May the fruit You find be love, joy, peace, patience, kindness, goodness, faithfulness, gentleness, and self-control. If what You find is not pleasing, prune me so I may grow and bloom into all You envision.

The LORD will guide you always; he will satisfy your needs in a sun-scorched land and will strengthen your frame. You will be like a well-watered garden, like a spring whose waters never fail. **Isaiah 58:11 NIV**

*H*is Reply

Stay close to the Source of your supply. Everything you need can be found in Me. I am the Living Water bringing life to your parched areas. I am the Light of the World, who brings new energy and hope into your darkness. I am the Bread of Life, feeding you all you need to grow and become stronger. I am the Sun of Righteousness, arising with healing and restoration. As you receive all I am, the fruit you bear will reflect what has been deposited inside you.

You will recognize them by their fruits. **Matthew 7:16 ESV**

Scripture: Song of Solomon 4:12-16

*G*oing **Deeper Questions:**

1. You are the Lord's private garden. What fundamental resources does every garden require to grow well?

2. When the spirit of the Lord blows upon His garden, a heavenly fragrance is released. What fruits are currently going in your garden? What fragrance is being released?

Simple Prayer: Blow upon my garden, Lord.

Day 77
Tear-Stained Joy

*Y*our **Heart's Cry**

Sitting in the pew with my hand clinching a tissue. I don't understand the physiological reasons, but Your presence floods my eyes with tears. Tears of peace, tears of hope, tears of relief. I feel secure in this new place in You, secure enough to release the hurt and let it flow freely. My tears betray the feelings I hold inside. I am not sad. I have finally found a place of reprieve. Yet, still they fall, one by one. A silent army carrying away years of burdens and years of pain. So I let them fall down my face, tear-stained and unashamed.

You have kept count of my tossings; put my tears in your bottle. Are they not in your book? **Psalm 56:8 ESV**

*H*is **Reply**

You are inestimably precious in My sight. You have broken open your alabaster box and washed Me with your tears. Each tear is a witness to the sorrow of the past. Each tear a reminder of the wounds and the pain. Not one is wasted. Not one is allowed to fall without recognition. I have collected them all. Each has been counted and recorded. Know your tears have a purpose. They have been planted in fertile ground. You have sown in tears, but you will reap in joy.

They shall come with weeping, And with supplications I will lead them. I will cause them to walk by the rivers of waters, In a straight way in which they shall not stumble. **Jeremiah 31:9 NKJV**

Scripture: Psalm 126:1-6

*G*oing **Deeper Questions:**

1. What are your feelings about crying? Do you view it as a positive or negative emotion, or is it a mixture of both?
2. How is crying part of the healing process? Can your tears be silent prayers?

Simple Prayer: Redeem my tears, Lord.

Day 78
Protection in the Storm

*Y*our Heart's Cry

Gray stratus clouds stand in the distance, growing more prominent as the day goes on. A rumbling fills the air, shaking the ground beneath it. Out of the corner of my eye, I see a flash of lightning pressing down hard against the Earth. As my grandma would say, "A storm's a comin'." We run to gather what we fear may be lost in the coming hours. All that is precious is brought inside. You see, we've seen what tornados can do. We've had life ripped up from under us. So, when the storms come, we run. We run hard to secure and defend what is ours. But, even our best preparation cannot compare to You. You are the fortress no storm can penetrate. You are the calm in the center of the chaos.

The disciples went and woke him, saying, "Master, Master, we're going to drown!" He got up and rebuked the wind and the raging waters; the storm subsided, and all was calm. **Luke 8:24 NIV**

*H*is Reply

I am your very present help in times of trouble. I will lift you up above the waves of frustration and helplessness that have tried to overwhelm you, and I will bring you to Myself and comfort you. Take time to quiet your mind and emotions in the midst of turmoil and demands, and I will give you peace in the midst of your own private storm. Refuse to be blown about by the winds of adversity by shifting your focus from the chaos and

self-preservation to concentrate on My words of promise. You must trust Me more than believing in the circumstances that shake you. Come into My rest and be restored in My presence. I am your safe harbor in the storms of life.

There will be a shelter to give shade from the heat by day, and refuge and protection from the storm and the rain. **Isaiah 4:6 NASB**

Scripture: Psalm 57:1-3

*G*oing **Deeper Questions:**

1. Protection is one of the wonderful promises found in the Word of God. What does it mean to be under the shadow of His wing? How is this a safe place when the storm is raging?

2. In Psalm 57, what does God send forth in verse 3? How are these two gifts part of life's storm shelter?

Simple Prayer: Be my shelter in the storm, Lord.

Day 79
The Mindful Path

*Y*our **Heart's Cry**

The battle rages in my mind. Daily choices present themselves to me, some good and some not. But You have made a way in the wilderness. You lead me to a place of purpose and passion. You make a way where there was no way. You have enlarged my path. My thoughts are filled with those things that are true and lovely. My thoughts are focused on You. My worries decrease in Your presence. My lack is filled. I am reminded of Whose I am. I am reminded of Your faithfulness and love.

Finally, brothers, whatever is true, whatever is honorable, whatever is just, whatever is pure, whatever is lovely, whatever is commendable, if there is any excellence, if there is anything worthy of praise, think about these things. **Philippians 4:8 ESV**

*H*is **Reply**

Submit your thoughts to Me. Seek Me in every situation. In the good times, seek Me, and in the difficult times, seek Me even more. I am here to reveal to you My glory. I am here to lead you out of the wilderness. When your mind turns to mumbling and complaining, turn and fix your eyes on Me. In praise and worship, you will find the cure for these wilderness mindsets. I have brought you out of the wilderness to never return. The wilderness had to give you up. You were not created to dwell in the wilderness. You were created for My glory. Become one with

My glory. Receive My thoughts and My mind. Allow who I am to remind you of who you are.

Do not be conformed to this world, but be transformed by the renewal of your mind, that by testing you may discern what is the will of God, what is good and acceptable and perfect. **Romans 12:2 ESV**

Scripture: Ephesians 4:17-24

Going Deeper Questions:

1. A calloused mind is one that is no longer able to change and be renewed. Look inwardly to see if there are any places in your thinking where you have become calloused. How does the truth in the Word of God work to restore and renew a calloused mind?

2. Putting on the new self is a choice. Just as you must choose what clothes you will wear today, you also get to choose what your response and attitude will be to your circumstances. What attitude will you choose today? Praise or pout? Worship or worry? Peace or panic? Love or lust? Joy or jealousy? Choose with a mind paved with truth.

Simple Prayer: Lord, transform me by the renewing of my mind.

Day 80
The Song of the Jubilant

*Y*our Heart's Cry

When I am weak, You are strong. There is only One who is worthy. So I will sing to the Lamb; You alone are worthy to receive all glory, all honor, and all power. You are worthy to save the lost. You are worthy to heal the wounded. You alone are worthy to lead Your beloved. I surrender my pain into Your hands. From this time forward, I will not look back at the pain that has paved my way to You. I reach out to touch the hem of Your garment. For You are the only One who can heal the losses I have suffered. I receive Your love with gratitude and joyous relief from the pain, guilt, and shame. I will sing a new song as the new creature I have become.

Taste and see that the LORD is good; blessed is the man who takes refuge in him. **Psalm 34:8 NIV**

*H*is Reply

Know I fight for you. I fight for your joy, your peace, your freedom, your song. Sing the song of the jubilant. Sing with abandon and liberty. Know you are loved with an everlasting love. Know that I am for you and not against you. Never will I leave or forsake you. I am with you always. You are never alone in this world. See the door I am holding open for you. Come up higher and sit with Me at the table of covenant. Be My guest at My table of blessing. I always have a seat reserved for you.

After this I looked, and there before me was a door standing open in heaven. And the voice I had first heard speaking to me like a trumpet said, 'Come up here, and I will show you what must take place after this.' **Revelation 4:1 NIV**

Scripture: Luke 8:43-48

*G*oing **Deeper Questions:**

1. Twelve years of disappointment. Twelve years of pain. Twelve years of pouring out with no tangible results. Then suddenly the season of discouragement was over, and a season of peace begun. What emotions do you believe this woman wrestled with as she made her way through the crowd? What emotions have you battled with over the past 50 days?

2. There is a reward for those who press in to touch Him. It is my prayer that you have experienced the goodness of God during your daily time of intimacy. What have you gained in the past 50 days? How is your relationship with God now compared to when you began? What is your Jubilee Challenge testimony? Share what God has done in your life at www.ComeEmpty.com.

Simple Prayer: Lord, You are my Healer and the Lifter of my head.

About the Author

*D*r. Saundra Dalton-Smith is a Board Certified internal medicine physician actively practicing in Alabama. She shares with audiences nationwide on the topics of eliminating limiting emotions, finding grace in difficult places, and experiencing personal renewal by drawing near to God. She is the founder of I Choose My Best Life, a movement to renew hope in a generation where depression, stress, and fear is peaking. Her other books include award-winning Set Free to Live Free: Breaking Through the 7 Lies Women Tell Themselves.

To book Saundra for your next retreat or conference, email her at: drdaltonsmith@IChooseMyBestLife.com

You can also follow Saundra on Twitter at: @DrDalton Smith or connect with her online at: www.facebook.com/IChooseMyBestLife or www.DrDaltonSmith.com

Topical Index

Made in the USA
Coppell, TX
06 November 2021